GET THE RIGHT JOB RIGHT NOW!

GET THE RIGHT JOB, RIGHT NOW!

*Proven Tools, Tips and Techniques
from Canada's Career Coach*

ALAN KEARNS

Collins

First edition

Published by Collins, an imprint of HarperCollins
Publishers Ltd.

HarperCollins Publishers Ltd
2 Bloor Street East, 20th Floor
Toronto, Ontario, Canada
M4W 1A8

www.harpercollins.ca

Library and Archives Canada Cataloguing in Publication

Kearns, Alan
Get the right job, right now! : proven tools, tips and
techniques from Canada's career coach / Alan Kearns. —
1st ed.

ISBN-13: 978-0-00-638662-9
ISBN-10: 0-00-638662-8

1. Vocational guidance—Canada. 2. Career development.
3. Career changes. 4. Job hunting. I. Title.

HF5382.5.C2K42 2007   650.14   C2006-905999-3

WEB 9 8 7 6 5 4 3 2 1

Printed and bound in Canada

For my family, with love

CONTENTS

LIST OF WORKSHEETS

To print out the worksheets listed above, or to access other job search tools, visit www.rightjob.ca.

LIST OF PODCASTS

To listen to the podcasts of the above interviews, as well as many more, visit www.rightjob.ca.

FOREWORD

You may find it ironic that a person who has built three Canadian job sites — Globecareers.com, Workopolis.com and Working.com — thinks that the key to a successful career is not found in searching job sites. Job sites are a great resource. But before you even log on to your computer, you have to do some soul-searching. I believe that the key to a successful career can only be found within you. Success comes from contributing to something you feel passionate about. So ask yourself: What makes you happy? What do you really like to do? It takes some self-reflection and analysis to find out what kind of work — and work environment — will be fulfilling for you. That may require trying out a few different types of jobs, from the hundreds of possibilities out there, to see what kind of work is right.

Once you have zeroed in on what kind of work you want, you have to do your research. Figure out what the company's business needs are and what you can do to help address them. What market is the company in? Where is it headed? Don't just focus on the job you are after, find out what other positions the company is hiring for; this will give you clues as to its future plans. If you do your homework and can talk about what a company needs and how your abilities can meet those demands, employers will take notice.

I know this from experience. My success to date has come from looking for opportunities to help grow the businesses that interested me. I studied the businesses and told them what I could do for their bottom lines. Even small changes that generate cost savings or new revenue can be of great interest — you don't have to know how to add millions of dollars. If you can help a company make money or save money, employers will be interested — it's what business is all about.

My first job after graduation was with Xerox, a company I had singled out as one I wanted to work for. I doggedly pursued that goal until the company hired me. Focusing on opportunities and on successfully executing plans to seize them were key factors in my creating Workopolis.com and Working.com.

I believe that you need to sell a company on what you *can* do, not what you have done in the past. Résumés alone can't tell people how you will perform. You will also need a cover letter, both to point out how your qualifications match the employer's requirements and to plant seeds in their minds about how you will approach the job. A professional and persuasive letter showcases your strengths as a candidate, explains why potential employers should meet you, and proves you're really interested in their company and what they have to offer.

Your experience will help clinch the deal. If you are entering a new field, don't hesitate to get some additional training to ease the transition to the kind of position you desire. There was a time when people could get by with the education and training they received at the beginning of their career, but that is no longer the case. Today, workers need to update their skills and knowledge continually in order to remain competitive and valuable in the workforce. It may take time, but it will pay off in the long run.

Ultimately, your success will come when you understand what drives you and when you are able to match your passions with the right opportunity. May the profiles you are about to read inspire you to great heights and happiness, and may Alan's expertise help you get the job you want.

KIM PETERS
General Manager, Working.com
Founding President of Workopolis.com
Toronto, 2007

INTRODUCTION

Recently, I sat down with a new client. She had spent thirteen years with her current employer, beginning as a manager and eventually rising to a very senior role. She had followed all the rules: obtained a great education, worked diligently, contributed in a number of meaningful ways, and given heart, body and mind to this national corporation.

She had decided to move farther out of town, so she asked her boss to allow her to telecommute three days a week. On a Saturday morning, after a long week of travelling for her organization, she received an e-mail from her boss flatly denying her request: not a phone call or the suggestion of a face-to-face discussion, but an e-mail!

Now she found herself at a crossroads, which was why she had come in to get my perspective. The e-mail from her boss had been a career tipping point, the final straw in her relationship with her company. "I want to find the right job" was her statement to me. Not only that, but she wanted the right job "right now."

Perhaps you recognize this scenario. You may have second-guessed your career — or yourself — and wondered what went wrong. Like my client, you may have been wrestling with that question for your whole career, only to one day receive an e-mail or have something else happen to change your relationship with your work, and you want to deal with the issue *immediately*. The status quo is no longer an option.

You have made a brave decision to begin a job search. This investment of money, time and energy is your first step on a long, winding, but ultimately rewarding road to greater career satisfaction. Job searching is a skill to be mastered, much like learning to swim or speak a second language.

This book contains time-tested methods, theories and tools that will yield successful results. Your job-search skill set will develop over time and with practice. Your first cover letter will not be as polished as your tenth, and the first interview will not go as smoothly as others later in the search. You may want the first job you apply for to be the perfect job; however, that is not realistic. Discovering the right job for you requires persistence and determination, and the utilization of all the tools and skills outlined in this success strategy. Every person who uses these tools will be at a different stage of his or her career journey, but these materials can be adapted to wherever you happen to be. If you know exactly which job you want to go after, skip over the modules you feel you do not need. Conversely, if you are unsure of where you are going, this curriculum will lead you through a comprehensive process that will allow you to identify your skills, talents, passions and desired lifestyle, and to find a job that fulfills you.

If you haven't yet found job satisfaction, you are not alone. We all confront challenges from time to time; this is part of the normal progression of any career. Managing your own career is difficult, but it becomes immeasurably easier to succeed — and enjoy yourself — once you understand and accept that there are no simple solutions.

Get the Right Job, Right Now! is a combination of my coaching methodology, practical tools and real-life coaching experience working with professionals from St. John's, Newfoundland, to Victoria, British Columbia. I have interviewed a number of successful Canadians, from Paul Henderson to Diane Francis, to seek advice drawn from their careers. Also included are the stories of a number of other Canadians who have been willing to share their experiences in their search for the right job. If you visit my website **www.rightjob.ca**, you can download podcasts of the career story interviews found in this book. You'll also find some useful worksheets and checklists to help you target and land that ideal career.

My hope is that you will take this resource and do something tangible with it, that reading this book and incorporating its principles will be like having me alongside you as your coach, twenty-four hours a day, 365 days a year. I cannot promise that if you complete all of the exercises in this book you will find the job of your dreams right away, but based on my experience and that of my clients, I am confident you will start to move in the right direction.

Along the road with you,

ALAN KEARNS
Ottawa, 2007

CHAPTER ONE

WHAT IS YOUR RIGHT JOB?

Many people languish in a job they hate or find unfulfilling, but this doesn't have to be your fate. The search for any job, especially the job of your dreams, requires dedication, drive and determination. So, let's get started. Think about your interests. What subjects did you love in school? Don't be alarmed if the answer to this question doesn't coincide exactly with what you are "best at." Here's an example: I had a friend who was a brilliant scientist, but she realized her true passion was British imperial history. She is now finishing her Ph.D. in history at Oxford. She doesn't know yet how she will apply her degree, but she *is* living her dream of studying history at the highest level. So, is your right job in a field similar to the one you are currently in, or is it in a totally different line of work?

Asking questions and getting insightful answers from Canadians is something that John Wright, senior vice-president of Ipsos-Reid, has been doing for most of his professional career. Ipsos-Reid is well-known for its election polls, but 99 percent of its work involves helping companies such as McDonald's, Coca-Cola and Wal-Mart to understand what is important to consumers. John's role, and that of his employer, is to bring context and perspective to these clients, thus enabling them to make smart decisions about new and existing brands and products.

I interviewed John to learn about his role and to hear his insights into the distinctly Canadian view of work. Ironically, the same things that apply to building one's career are the things that help sell dog food. A research company provides its clients with a valuable perspective and framework, and companies then adapt their products and services to reflect their understanding of the current market.

Similarly, individual employees need to put the current employment market into context in order to make intelligent choices about their own careers. Those who research the market and gain an understanding of it will be best prepared for the realities they encounter.

Ten years ago, more than 36 percent of Canadians feared for their jobs; today, only 12 percent do. Today, 19 percent of Canadians feel less loyal toward their employer than they did ten years ago, while 22 percent feel more loyal. Unlike back then, the major challenges confronting employers today are how to attract and retain qualified employees. In some parts of Canada, companies are desperate for skilled employees, and even in low-paying sectors such as retail, employers are having a very difficult time hiring staff.

The economy is always cyclical; there will be times when it is red-hot and the right job is easy to find, just as job searches will be tougher when we're experiencing a downturn. But despite the economic conditions, the best people will always be in demand. Being the best at what you do is the greatest advantage you can gain in order to shield yourself from changes in the economic climate.

In my opinion, few people become experts at the career journey. You may end up with one career that is thirty-five years in the making, or with several careers. Your first career may go well, with only a few ups and downs, or you may invest your time in several unsatisfying careers before you land in the right one. What is critically important is that you keep your work experience in context and be pragmatic about it.

LEONARD LEE: THE PHASES OF A CAREER

"I paid attention to what I did like and what I didn't like, and have built my career around the things I like."

Before founding Lee Valley Tools, Leonard Lee was a civil servant for more than seventeen years. He worked for the Canadian Department of Industry as a trade commissioner, first in Chicago, then in Peru. When he came back from Peru to settle in Ottawa and work with the federal government, he struggled to find his niche. What troubled him was that more and more of his colleagues were literally counting down the years, months and days until they could retire — in a sense, they were living for retirement. For Leonard, the office felt more like a penal colony than a productive, healthy work environment.

The Start-Up Phase

In the late 1970s, Leonard wanted a barrel stove kit to heat one of the buildings on the farm he owned. He wound up putting together a stove kit that he could sell to others. During his first winter in business, he broke even. He was quite pleased with this result, particularly in light of the high start-up costs and the uniqueness of his product. Still, he didn't immediately quit his day job; he waited for the business to grow .

Woodworking was Leonard's hobby, so he began to stock the specialized tools that do-it-yourselfers and gardeners seek out. In 1978, he mortgaged his home and put together a mail-order catalogue that went out that fall. By December, the business was profitable. This was good news not only for him and his wife, but for the two employees he'd hired, who were understandably concerned about the stability of their jobs. They need not have worried. Today, Lee Valley Tools employs almost 900 people.

The guiding principle of Lee Valley Tools was to be the kind of company that ordinary people would like to deal with, and the kind of company that treated customers the way Leonard himself liked to be treated. There really is no secret to the success of Lee Valley; Leonard simply knew his market. The customer base grew quickly, mainly through word of mouth. Out of necessity, Leonard spent very little money marketing the business. The company's growth surprised many observers, but surprised its founder even more.

The Momentum Phase

When the business grew to twelve employees, things suddenly became very difficult. Leonard says wryly that he felt like a mother sow. "Every time I moved, I took twelve people with me," he notes.

He surmounted this problem by first setting out to find a general manager and then other top people to help him run his business. (Ironically, he says he has had an easier time running a company with close to 900 employees than with only twelve.) This support freed Leonard up to spend time on the catalogue — designing, selecting and testing products and writing catalogue copy.

"It is not what a president normally does, but it was what I wanted to do and what I was best at," he says.

Leonard paid attention to what he liked doing and what he didn't like doing, and shaped his job description accordingly. His passion and his desire for learning even led him to write a best-selling book on tool sharpening.

After eight years, he hired a trustworthy chief financial officer to deal with banking, budgets and cash flow. Leonard didn't even sign cheques anymore.

As the company grew, he stayed with it because he loved the business and truly enjoyed being a part of it. Indeed, he was afraid to retire, but in time he felt he had to step down.

"I was getting older, I wasn't getting any better, and I had to leave," he says.

Leonard recognized that he needed to pass on the reins to his son. Otherwise, the company would be held back by his limitations.

The Regeneration Stage

Leonard's retirement, which began just short of his sixty-fifth birthday, didn't last long. One of his friends was a surgeon who enjoyed using

Lee Valley's products. In fact, he was using a Lee Valley tool as a scalpel in the operating room, since it was superior to anything commercially available to surgeons!

This friend approached Leonard to ask if it was possible to produce a superior scalpel for surgeons. This was just the kind of challenge that Leonard needed.

A new business was born: Canica is the company that Leonard and his friend created to design medical instruments. Leonard is in charge of a company again, this time with sixteen employees. The company is four years old, but it has taken a lot longer to grow because it is such a new industry.

Still, says Leonard Lee, "It is more complex and satisfying to design and build tools that improve people's health."

THE CAREER EQUATION: FIVE KEY COMPONENTS TO YOUR CAREER IDENTITY

There is a famous quote: "Do what you love and the money will follow." However, in the model that I have developed, I think you need to look at the whole picture, not just what you love — or money. The career equation is a valuable tool for assessing your career identity and job satisfaction. What is this equation?

Talents + Passions + Values + Lifestyle + Ecosystem = Job Satisfaction

Is your current job making full use of your talents? Igniting your passions? Is it in line with your values and allowing you your desired lifestyle? The career equation should be posted where you can see it throughout your job search. It should also be revisited every six months or so.

Talents

My goal is to get you to the point where you are utilizing your talents at least 60 percent of the time. Before I go any further, we need to be sure we understand the difference between talents and skills, both of which we have to use in our work. To put it simply, talents are those things that come naturally and that you really enjoy doing. Skills, on the other hand, are what you gain through training and experience. You'll tend to derive a minimum amount of satisfaction when you are using your skills. Every person that I've interviewed for this book has found a place in the world of work where they can use their *talents*. People don't always fully appreciate their talents; they write them off as "just something I do." But in my experience, talent is something the market never has enough of. There are many who are skilled, but few are truly talented at what they are doing — or doing what they are talented at. During your day, pay attention to the tasks that you are working on, and use these three questions as a way of identifying talents:

- Does time go by quickly during the task?
- Are you energized by it?
- Do you get consistent positive feedback on the results?

If the answer is yes to all three questions, you are talented at those tasks.

If you can spend more than 60 percent of your time in your "talent zone," the market will recognize this and will offer you long-term job security. The world needs more of your talents and less of your skills!

You have to have a natural ability to do something well. When you are in your talent zone, great things happen.

Passions

It sounds obvious, but it's essential to choose the place where you will be happiest. If you like what you are doing, you will do a better job than if you're working passionlessly for nothing other than money. The odds of success are greater if you focus on self-expansion rather than self-interest. Passion is both the fuel and the focus. It energizes you and encourages you to learn. If you are engaged by what you do, it will be very difficult to fail.

Values

Values are defined as "the accepted principles or standard of an individual or group."

Each of us has a unique value system that guides us to make decisions and take action in ways that allow us to sleep well at night. If your values are out of line with your work, you will struggle to meet standards and expectations. You must pay attention to personal values (how you treat yourself) and corporate values (how you treat your managers or employees).

Lifestyle

Here, "lifestyle" describes how well you integrate your skills into your life. Don't be trapped into chasing the highest salary offered; look instead for the more interesting job. In case after case, you will see that those who are most successful tend to start out with a salary on the lower end of their lifestyle needs. However, if they are truly passionate about what they do, they'll eventually rise to the top tier in that sector in terms of salary. Ultimately, lifestyle evolves out of being true to yourself and choosing opportunities that best fit your needs.

Ecosystem

In gardening, you need a good ecosystem to raise healthy plants. Your career also needs a healthy ecosystem to flourish. A career ecosystem consists of more than just the company culture; it includes the location, physical space, peers, work hours, size of company, opportunity for growth and, perhaps most important, leadership. If you have had a great boss, you'll know the difference that an effective leader makes in terms of creating a work environment. When one element of the ecosystem is altered, it changes everything.

OPPORTUNITY ANALYSIS

The Career Equation Tool

List your talents, passions, values, and elements of your ideal lifestyle and employment ecosystem. Include as many of each as you can think of; they don't have to be work-related — everything is relevant.

- **Talents:** What are you good at? What do others say your talents are? (Examples: writing, drawing, knack with children, problem solving, building things, conceptualizing.)
- **Passions:** What do you feel passionate about? What do you love? What is important to you? (Examples: food, your family, working outdoors, faith, ideas, finding out how things work.)
- **Values:** What are your personal values? What do you value in other people? What do believe strongly in? (Examples: family, faith, caring, security, trust.)
- **Lifestyle:** What do you enjoy about your current lifestyle? What would be your ideal lifestyle? (Examples: large home, large income, having a cottage on a lake, x number of children, education.)
- **Ecosystem:** What kind of an environment do you work well in? (Examples: positive, creative, teamwork, cubicle or open concept.)

Now that you have compiled your various lists, look at each individual one and rank each of your talents, passions, values, lifestyle and parts of the ecosystem. Consider why one may be more important to you than another. Use these lists to rate your current job and each of your past positions on how well your talents, passions, etc., were utilized. Use a scale from 1 to 10, with 10 meaning the job made full use of everything on your lists, and 1 meaning that the job did not meet any of the criteria on the list.

Complete this chart for *each* relevant position you have held:

CAREER EQUATION CHART	
Job Title/Position:	
Talents	Criteria Met: • • • Score: /10
Passions	Criteria Met: • • • Score: /10
Values	Criteria Met: • • • Score: /10
Lifestyle	Criteria Met: • • • Score: /10
Ecosystem	Criteria Met: • • • Score: /10

Now for each job:

- Add up the score in each individual category, to a maximum of 10 (10 being highest).
- Add up each of the five categories, for a maximum score per job of 50 (50 being highest).
- Evaluate each job for its numerical fit and consider some of

the trends that have been occurring within your career journey up until this point.

Here are the results for your scores:

Under 30: Unacceptable situation. What action do you need to take immediately?

30 to 35: Needs improvement. What is your lowest score?

36 to 40: Good. Where are the low and high scores?

Above 40: Right job. What areas can you improve upon?

If you consistently scored high in talents and passions and low in values and ecosystem, then you are most likely in the right job but in the wrong company. You should start the journey towards finding a company that is much better suited to you.

If you scored high in values and ecosystem but low in talents and passions, you are in the right company but the wrong job. You might consider how to shift within your organization to an area that is a better fit.

If you scored low in all areas, you need to look at both your career choice and the company that you are employed by; the right fit doesn't exist in any area.

Take note of themes and trends within each of the categories. For example, imagine that one of your natural talents is musical ability. If in each of your past positions that talent scored low, it's clear that you were unable to use your musical talent in those jobs. You may determine that you value this talent in yourself, and should perhaps be looking for different ways to express it.

When the process is complete, think about what you have learned from this exercise. What information do you take away, both personally and in regards to your career? Does your current job measure up? If not, you might consider making a change for the better. But before you can confidently decide to stay or go, you must answer this question honestly: "Why do I want to leave?" Are you running from problems you carry to every job? If so, a new job is not going to solve those problems, and you might do well to seek the assistance of a trained psychologist in defining and understanding these problems and working through them. If, on the other hand, you conclude that you need greater job satisfaction or more appropriate compensation, a job search is a distinct possibility.

A job search may also be called for when you reach a career tipping point. This can come from within: you've become frustrated and have started to distance yourself from your work, or you've hit a plateau in terms of job satisfaction and are no longer as willing to go the extra mile. Or you don't feel challenged or appreciated, or you sense that you are underpaid. You may believe that you have accomplished as much as you possibly can in your current job and are no longer growing in it, or that your life has changed to the point that your job no longer meshes with your talents, passions, values or lifestyle. The impetus might also be external: your industry may be changing in ways that don't seem to favour the sort of work you currently do. Perhaps you are getting clear signals that your employer is dissatisfied with your work — for instance, a less-than-stellar performance review. Or a promotion you expected and thought you deserved was given to a co-worker. Or you must report to a new boss. Or the company has appointed a new board, and you don't agree with the direction they are taking.

The Right Job Checklist

Now that you have organized your top five elements for each of the categories (talents, passions, values, lifestyle and ecosystem), you should have a total of twenty-five distinctive elements that would be part of your ideal job.

The next step is to narrow these down further to the top ten elements you are looking for. You can choose these from any of the categories. This becomes your Right Job Checklist. Don't let fear or pragmatism get the upper hand here; listen to your gut as well as your head. Once you have chosen ten elements, rank them. And don't over-analyze your choices — put them in the order that seems most accurate. Feel free to run this checklist by a few friends who know you well to get their feedback and determine whether your self-analysis is correct.

RIGHT JOB CHECKLIST

List, in order of importance, the top ten elements you are looking for in your dream job.

1. _____
2. _____
3. _____
4. _____
5. _____
6. _____
7. _____
8. _____
9. _____
10. _____

DEBBIE TRENHOLM: USING AN MBA TO UNCORK YOUR CAREER

"Where do I fit? In my heart of hearts it wasn't going to be high-tech as my next step."

Debbie graduated with a Bachelor of Arts in Political Science and French on a Saturday, and by Monday afternoon she had an interview with Corel Corporation. By six o'clock that same day Debbie had an offer, and on Tuesday she began her career as employee #200. Her roles in the company evolved until she became responsible for building market share with business partners in England, Ireland and Scandinavia, spending half her time in Ottawa and the other half in Europe. Later, she moved to a startup, FastLane Technologies — this time as employee #60 — liaising with other business partners, such as IBM and Hewlett-Packard. FastLane existed for roughly three years, growing to 300 employees, before it was acquired by the California company Quest Software.

Debbie was doing well at Quest, but she was getting restless. She had always planned on getting a master's degree, and so she chose to pursue the Executive MBA program at the Queen's School of Business. This allowed her to pursue an MBA while still working; at the same time, it gave her the opportunity to consider a career in another industry.

Debbie was tempted to stay in the high-tech sector, although she wasn't completely comfortable there. "Where do I fit? Where can I find a personal challenge and where could my experience help another company? In my heart of hearts, it wasn't going to be high-tech as my next step."

She'd always been passionate about wine, had taken courses and had even become a sommelier. Given her international experience along with her creativity and marketing background, it seemed to her that the wine industry might be her "fit."

Debbie decided to test the waters by doing her MBA internship in a winery. As a result, she gained valuable insights and created networking opportunities, all without quitting her day job. Her passion for wine grew, and it became obvious that the business of wine was the right fit for her.

Once she had finished her MBA, Debbie quit her high-tech job and spent some time exploring European wineries while she brushed up on her French, trained for a half-marathon and recharged her mental batteries, all this to prepare for the task of building her next career.

With the goal of taking the mystery out of wine, she used some savings to launch her own company, The Savvy Grapes. Starting small and keeping her overhead low, she began offering wine classes and tastings and a wine subscription service. She also helped restaurants develop their wine lists and pitched her marketing and business-development expertise to wineries. At first, she marketed her business to her existing network, but she was always on the lookout for opportunities to broaden her clientele.

Debbie built her business by being constantly creative and by defining which aspects of her business were personally most satisfying as well as profitable. She took a huge and very successful leap, and the MBA program and internship helped her make a career change.

"If you think you can do it, give it a try, if you can arrange your life or your work to test it and see if you would like it better. It will be exhausting for the first while, but it will help you to investigate, validate and become confident that you are making the right decision."

In defining the criteria for your right job, you need to balance your talents, passions, values, desired lifestyle and ecosystem. Remember the career equation: Talents + Passions + Values + Lifestyle + Ecosystem = The Right Job. If any of these elements should go out of balance, your level of job satisfaction will change.

There are many important aspects to a career: earnings, location, roles, benefits, working from home vs. in an office, the hours, management style—in addition to the five elements listed above. They all matter when you set out to define your right job.

How does the right job you have just created compare with the career equation? Is your right job in line with your talents, values and personality? If there are glaring discrepancies, return to the previous tools and shape the aspects of your right job so that they become more in line with what you discovered about yourself earlier.

CHAPTER TWO

KNOW THYSELF

Do you know who you are from a career perspective? It sounds like a very simple question, yet it is one of the most difficult to answer. However, finding that answer will give you one of the most powerful tools with which to shape your future.

Over the next few pages, you will complete exercises designed to help you define and understand your job history. The exercises may shed light on why you have ended up in jobs that haven't been as satisfying as you had hoped. Finally, you will be guided through the process of identifying specific career and life goals that will allow you to balance potential jobs with how well they fit your needs as a worker and an individual.

YOUR PERSONAL HISTORY

Think about the significant people and events that have influenced your education and career choices. Now list them chronologically, from your earliest job or education memory to the present. The entries on your list can be positive or negative, but you need to write them down. For instance:

> When I was thirteen I loved writing. My teacher, Ms. X, said that I wasn't a very imaginative writer. I was crushed. I stopped writing for fun.
>
> My first job, when I was fifteen, was working with disadvantaged teenagers. My boss, Harvey, was great because he always took the time to listen to all his staff, even the part-time students. He made us believe our opinions were important.

Evaluation

Your reaction to this list of significant people and events may stir up negative memories as well as positive ones. You will also, upon analysis, discover turning points in your career and education choices. Focus on the events and people again, and this time, place a descriptive symbol beside each one, as follows: mark negative effects as (–), positive as (+), turning point as (T), and no reaction as (o).

Review the list and note the connections between the different people, events and experiences. What do these connections mean to you? Reflecting on your education and work experiences will help you understand the decisions you've made and the ramifications those decisions have had on your life journey. This awareness will provide you with a foundation upon which to start building a new career. When you do this exercise, keep in mind the key elements for career joy: talents, passions, values, lifestyle and ecosystem.

Patterns

Are there any underlying patterns in your work history? Are there recognizable environments in which you felt job satisfaction, whether because of situations, work colleagues or employers? What makes your positive experiences better than the negative ones you have noted? How have both kinds of experiences shaped your career choices? (For example, perhaps your first job experience was a positive one because of a great boss, not because of the work you were doing.)

Next, think about your family's job history. You may not have realized the impact that your family can have on your job history. A study conducted in 1999 concluded that nine out of ten children felt some need to demonstrate competence in order to earn or deserve parental love. For most people, this pattern continues into adulthood: they use their careers to seek approval from loved ones, despite the anxiety and disappointment this pattern can produce.

Trace the career history of your family and place it into a "tree" chart format for visualization. List each family member's job, education, talents, values and definition of career success. Include your grandparents, your parents, your siblings, yourself, your spouse and your in-laws (if applicable). Feel free to include non–family members who acted as mentors or had a significant impact on you.

CAREER FAMILY TREE

Maternal Grandmother

Job	
Education	
Talents	
Values	
Career Success	

Maternal Grandfather

Job	
Education	
Talents	
Values	
Career Success	

Paternal Grandfather

Job	
Education	
Talents	
Value	
Career Success	

Paternal Grandmother

Job	
Education	
Talents	
Value	
Career Success	

Mother

Job	
Education	
Talents	
Values	
Career Success	

Father

Job	
Education	
Talents	
Values	
Career Success	

Yourself

Job	
Education	
Talents	
Values	
Career Success	

Sibling 1

Job	
Education	
Talents	
Values	
Career Success	

Sibling 2

Job	
Education	
Talents	
Values	
Career Success	

Sibling 3

Job	
Education	
Talents	
Values	
Career Success	

Partner

Job	
Education	
Talents	
Values	
Career Success	

Partner's Family History
Mother

Job	
Education	
Talents	
Values	
Career Success	

Father

Job	
Education	
Talents	
Values	
Career Success	

Additional People of Influence (family, friends, mentors, etc.)

Job	
Education	
Talents	
Values	
Career Success	

Job	
Education	
Talents	
Values	
Career Success	

After you have completed the exercise, consider these questions:

- Who in your career tree are you most like?
- Who do you feel has influenced you the most — both professionally and personally (positively or negatively)?
- Did you have discussions around work in your family?
- What were your relatives' views and values about work?
- Did your family achieve their personal and professional goals from their work?
- How was success defined by your family?
- What were your family's views about failure?
- How do your family and friends view your work situation now?
- What needs, if any, are you supposed to be fulfilling for your family in your present career?
- Are there themes among the individuals on your career tree? Do you fit into any of these themes?
- What have you learned from this exercise? What information have you taken away, both personally and in regards to your career?

JOANNA TRACK: FINDING YOUR OWN SWEET SPOT

"I had a very roundabout way of finding my own sweet spot. Getting there, work-wise and life-wise, happened by marrying all the things that are important to me: a creative team, an environment that I love and working in an area of passion..."

With a degree in math, Joanna considered a career in finance and started down that track in an MBA program. After working in bond trading at Merrill Lynch, "it was becoming clear to me that finance was not my path."

In the second year of her MBA, Joanna dropped all her finance courses and instead took courses in strategy, marketing and operations. It was becoming clearer to her that she was leaning towards marketing. She joined The Loyalty Group, operators of the Air Miles program, as an analyst. "This was the best thing for me. It mixed analysis with creativity." After that she spent six years at OgilvyOne, the direct-marketing division of the advertising agency Ogilvy & Mather. For Joanna, direct marketing was the perfect blend — it involved respecting and valuing the importance of branding while being directly involved with consumer-based businesses.

Returning to Canada after some time in New York, Joanna realized that she didn't want to stay in advertising. While working in New York she had come across an e-newsletter called *Dailycandy*, which alerted readers to the newest and hippest products and services the city had to offer. It had a conversational tone, like two friends talking about a great new store or restaurant or the coolest pair of jeans. She loved the newsletter, and realized there was nothing like it in Toronto. With her background in marketing and business, she sensed an opportunity and decided to give it a go.

Joanna arranged to work part-time for OgilvyOne on a contract, which enabled her to devote her energies to starting up Sweetspot. "I had a big idea, but I didn't try and execute it all at once." Joanna focused on the Toronto market and grew the business organically with the help of freelancers and people she knew from her marketing network. The site quickly took off, and within two years she had opened in Montreal, Vancouver and Calgary. Along the way she confronted challenges ranging from cash flow to working time. She used up her RRSPs — every dollar she had. "The cost is quite high and the sacrifice is more than you think."

Meanwhile, Rogers Publishing had been watching Joanna, having become interested in her business model. "I had worked over two years under a lot of stress and with all the challenges of a small business. I was tired and looking for a partner." Rogers made a strategic investment, offering Joanna the best of both worlds: access to capital and some of the top publishing experts in Canada, while she maintained editorial autonomy. "Finding my sweet spot, both work-wise and life-wise, happened by marrying all the things that are important to me: a creative team and environment, and working in an area of passion, supported by the Rogers group."

Joanna's success has not come without personal cost. "You have to decide what you want and what you are willing to trade," she says. But "if you know what you want and you put the effort in, you will get it."

Ultimately, you must ask yourself, Are you getting what you want from work? If not, why? This is a tough question to answer honestly, but you need to take the time to answer it thoroughly. As a coach, I help clients to clarify their personal situations. I work with them to determine what they want from their work, and develop a plan to help them achieve their goals. In order to find your right job, you need to understand and identify what you want from that right job. Your right job will not be the same as the one for the person who sits beside you on the bus. Understanding what you want is a key ingredient in finding a good fit.

WHO AM I?

I frequently discuss issues of identity with clients. To some extent, our work defines us — for better or for worse. When we meet someone new, the second question we ask after their name is almost always "What do you do for a living?" I believe the questions we are really asking are: How important are you? What purpose do you have? How do I relate to or classify you? The thing to remember is that the work we do is correlated with who we are, but *we are not our work.* Our identity comes out of our talents, values and strengths.

People who lose sight of that fact are highly likely to experience an identity crisis if they happen to be laid off. Because they derive their purpose from what they do for work, the loss of a job leads to a loss of identity. The challenge is to keep work and life balanced — and separate. Therefore, if we are laid off — or even if we are experiencing a rough patch at work — we will be better equipped to handle it.

By avoiding the temptation to define yourself by your work, you will be empowered to manage your career more effectively; if things go well, you will experience more joy; if things *don't* go your way, the personal pain you suffer won't be as deep. The ultimate form of job security is knowing who you are and what you have to offer the world of work.

Some final thoughts from David Whyte: "One of the outer qualities of great captains, great leaders and great bosses is that they are unutterably themselves." It is important to be yourself, and being yourself requires that you know who you are. Out of this self-knowledge comes great work and a great life. At the core of what I do for my clients is getting a true sense of who they are. Once this is clear, the work options come easily into focus.

GOAL SETTING

Now, take the knowledge you have gained in the first steps of this chapter and define specific objectives. List them and use them as a guide when you consider different jobs. Being joyful requires that you strike a balance among various aspects of your life. These include:

- physical (healthy eating, exercise, rest)
- mental (challenges, learning, imagination)
- emotional (feelings of belonging, security, love)
- philosophical (spirituality, meaning, attitudes, purpose)
- social (family, community, friends)
- career (money, fulfillment)
- recreational (play, leisure, vacation)

Many people place too much weight on the career aspect, thus creating an imbalance in their lives overall. But a fulfilling job alone does not make for a complete life. A job is what you *do*; it is not who you *are*.

Consider the various aspects of your life by completing the following chart.

MY PERSONAL, CAREER AND LIFE OBJECTIVES
Complete the following statements:
The dreams I have for my life are
My career goals: The work I would like to be doing in five years is
The work I would like to be doing in two and a half years is
The work I would like to be doing right now is
My physical objectives are
My mental objectives are
My emotional objectives are
My philosophical objectives are
My social objectives are
My financial and lifestyle objectives are
My recreational objectives are
Skills I would like to develop are
Organizations and people I would like to support more are

JEN RILEY: BUILDING YOUR BRAND IN THE BIG LEAGUES

"Being part of something bigger than me is interesting to see. The corporate benefits at EA are really great. There are endless possibilities; you get to create your own career and build your own brand."

Ever since Jen was young she wanted to become a sports journalist. She played volleyball at Queen's University. Her passion for sports and her creativity got her a job right out of university at WTSN (the women's sports network) and then shortly afterwards at TSN. She was doing a lot of the research and writing for the anchors and thought she was on the fast track to the anchor desk. TSN saw her potential, but they had just hired a female anchor; if she was going to get on-camera experience, she would have to go to smaller markets.

So, she quit TSN and headed west. She attended nineteen job interviews in eight days, covering most of the small outlets across western Canada. Jen was the runner-up for a number of jobs, but didn't succeed in landing an anchor position, so she decided to create a job of her own. She launched her own outdoor lifestyle show, *The Vibe Outside*, lining up a number of investors and producing ten shows for local TV in Whistler. Jen's writing and producing skills developed, and she started to get some national attention. She lined up sponsorship from a major advertising partner and had an agreement with a national broadcaster. However, the deal fell apart at the last minute. "This was my quarter-life crisis," she says. "Everyone needs a big failure to recover from ... this was mine."

From the *Vibe Outside* experience, she learned how much she loved to strategize, write and promote. She also realized that her home was in Vancouver — this was a big turn for her. By now, she knew that she didn't want to do another startup and that she didn't want to focus on sports broadcasting anymore. Through coaching and her own experience, Jen discovered that public relations was the direction she wanted to go in. "I knew that I would be good at it. Even though I had this failure, I had learned a whole lot and was confident in what I could do."

Jen got a role as the PR person for the Whistler Film Festival. She created her own promotional package and started to network within the sports community in Vancouver. She did some freelance work with the U.S. network ESPN and happened to spend a day at Electronic Arts (EA), one of the world's largest and most successful makers of gaming software, with an NBA athlete. She met the PR team and mentioned that she was focusing on PR and that they were a company that she was interested in. A week later, a vacancy opened up at the company, and Jen gave EA a call. They remembered her, and she was quickly hired. "Much of my job [involves] pitching a story that the sports media wants. I have a pretty good sense of this from all of my experience."

Jen works hard — she gets home at 7:00 p.m — but says it doesn't feel like work. Her philosophy is not to give up. The occasional dip in the road is important, because the high points look that much higher.

"I feel very lucky to be where I am and to have some failures behind me. My journey wasn't the straight path that I might have expected when I graduated. The one thread from the beginning has been my network, mentors and support group — people that I have learned from ... It was the biggest factor in my career success: keep in contact and learn, learn, learn! That gets you to the right career."

YOUR CAREER BALANCE SHEET

When corporate executives want a snapshot of their companies' financial health, they consult the balance sheet. This next tool will help you compile your personal career balance sheet. In this case, your assets consist of your skills, talents and experiences, while your liabilities could include areas of underdevelopment such as education, employment and low self-confidence. By taking stock of your assets and setting goals to turn your liabilities into areas of growth, you will greatly improve your chances of getting hired.

MY CAREER BALANCE SHEET	
Assets (skills, experiences)	Liabilities (growth areas)

Consider the items you have listed as liabilities on your personal career balance sheet. What can you do to overcome them?

RESEARCHING JOB TITLES

Research is invaluable to a job search or a successful career transition. It reduces risk, increases options and improves the quality of your decision-making. Now that you have a sense of your talents, values, personality characteristics and goals, you can begin researching a series of job titles that may pique your interest and give you an idea of which areas to pursue.

You may think that you don't know where to begin, but don't panic: the most important thing is simply to get started. Bear in mind that research is not deciding, it's exploring. The ultimate goal is to find a job that will be a perfect fit, but don't expect to find it right away — give yourself the time you need to conduct this search properly. Remember your first round of golf or game of tennis, or your first time on a bike? It took time to learn the skills and improve. Finding the right job will similarly be an ongoing process.

This is my "walk, don't run" advice: think of this exercise as research *towards* an answer. If you get too focused on the "answer" at this stage, you may miss out on some options that might arise. Start an opportunity file where you can put your ideas, articles and job postings. Keep it in a convenient spot on your desk or carry it with you. When you revisit this file in a few weeks, you may become aware of some ideas that you originally overlooked.

Join some new networks: get involved in anything from volunteering to politics. These new venues will bring you into contact with professionals in different careers and companies. At the same time, look to your past: catch up with old university and high school friends. This is another terrific way to regenerate your network and expose yourself to new career ideas.

Keep in mind your career investment. How much time, money and resources are you willing to invest in making the transition to the right job? The more of these you devote to your search, the wider the range of career options will be.

Here are some websites to help you research the marketplace. With more than 30,000 different jobs to choose from, it's clear that your goal should not be to explore all of them. This part of the process is, however, designed to encourage you to keep an open and curious mind. Don't be afraid to broaden your scope, because you can always narrow the list down at the proper time.

www.jobsetc.ca
This website, which uses a quiz-based tool to generate career ideas, is helpful when you have no real clear sense of what career you are looking for. The quiz takes about fifteen minutes.

www.jobfutures.ca
This website will generate a list of job titles based upon areas of interest. It is helpful when you have a broader understanding of your skill set and are looking for job titles that match the way you are naturally wired.

www23.hrdc-drhc.gc.ca
This website is great if you have an area that you are specifically focused on. It offers a comprehensive list of roles by job category, and is helpful for narrowing down your career options.

strategis.ic.gc.ca

This site is useful for researching businesses, trends and the economic overviews of a sector. It is also useful if you are thinking about relocating.

www.statcan.ca

The Statistics Canada website is a terrific site that provides a great amount of information on all aspects about geography, employment and salary trends.

www.jobprofiles.org

This site gives you clear descriptions of job titles, the specifics of each title involved and a thorough overview of education options.

www.edu.gov.on.ca/eng/career/

This website provides an overview of programs offered through colleges and universities that can prepare you for specific careers. It also provides links to most of the professional career associations.

www.canlearn.ca

Another educational website that provides a comprehensive list of resources for adults and students, this site has helpful information related to scholarships, universities and colleges.

www.canadian-universities.net

This site offers a comprehensive list of universities and colleges in Canada. It also provides an extensive overview of Master's and MBA programs.

www.careeredge.ca

If you are looking for an internship, this is a good Canadian resource for connecting with employers who are looking for interns.

www.salaryexpert.com
This site provides both Canadian and American salary reports, broken down by sectors and roles. This will help you determine what people in different industries are paid and, therefore, how much you can expect to make.

ANDREW STEWART: THE SINGING SOLICITOR ON THE ROAD TO PASSION

"You have to follow what is in your heart, guide it with what is in your head and listen to your inner voice."

Despite a Master's of Law from Cambridge and a successful law career at two firms in Vancouver, Andrew didn't love the law. He was stressed out and anxious and felt that he wasn't living up to his own standards.

Andrew had pursued law in university as a route to a secure career, but he had always been interested in music. He decided to make a change and focus on what he really loved: the performing arts. He left the law firm and went into private practice to gain more control and flexibility over his schedule. He started to sing again and took voice lessons and acting classes at night. As he started to listen to his inner voice — putting to rest the inner turmoil he'd felt as a result of his dissatisfaction with his legal career — his singing voice got stronger. He had found the place where his passion and his desire for excellence worked in harmony.

Andrew spent a year studying with Peter Barcza, a baritone with a worldwide reputation. He was offered a role by Nancy Hermiston, the director of opera at the University of British Columbia. A series of other roles followed. He also auditioned successfully for the internationally recognized two-year diploma program in opera offered through UBC's School of Music. It was a challenging time, as Andrew was still in private practice, this time studying opera by day and doing work in corporate finance law at night.

When he completed the opera program, Andrew had a choice to make: should he pursue opera full time and try to take it to the next level? In 2006, he won a coveted spot in the Canadian Opera Company's Studio Ensemble program, which grooms singers to become world-class performers. The program draws hundreds of applicants from around the world, and Andrew was one of only three to be chosen as a resident artist.

Andrew has learned that you need to listen to yourself and find your own voice. "Sometimes we are telling ourselves what we should do. It is important to do what you want to do *now*. It's good to be sensible, but listen to that voice. You have to follow what is in your heart, guide it with what is in your head and listen to your inner voice."

Where Am I Headed?

Developing a clear sense of where you want to go, and drawing up a practical plan of how to get there, is fundamental to managing your career. Few of us will get this understanding at a very young age; for most, the question "Where am I headed?" will be revisited time and again. It will be an ongoing process.

CHAPTER THREE

BASIC JOB-SEARCH SKILLS

O ne of the key things to consider as you begin your job search is your mindset, your level of confidence. How you feel about your skill set and what you have to offer is the first and most important concern as you set out to find the right job.

Peter Jensen is a performance psychologist who has been working with Canada's Olympic program for many years. While other coaches focus on technical skills, Peter helps athletes to prepare mentally. In 2002 and 2006, he helped the Canadian women's hockey team, which won gold medals at the Winter Olympics. Despite the common stereotype, there is no such thing as a dumb jock: most athletes are disciplined, talented and intelligent — they have to be in order to reach their goals. In fact, the skills that a person develops on the playing field are applicable to the work world. In sport, as in work:

- your performance is measured
- you are under tremendous pressure
- there is uncertainty over an event's outcome (that is, nobody ultimately knows who is going to win or lose)
- there is a heightened sense of excitement or even anxiety over the importance of an upcoming competition
- you sometimes have to make do with fewer people or resources than you'd like
- you are now facing a global playing field of competition (akin to the World Cup or the Olympics)

Job-search success and career management are about the internal advantages that get you, the player, to excel in your chosen career.

At the world-class level, most working professionals have the same technical and strategic advantages at their disposal. However, the "internal advantage" is what will put you over the top and provide you with the greatest opportunity to win. You choose what level you want to perform at, especially in today's work environment. To use a hockey analogy, you can choose to watch the clock and use your ice time without feeling any motivation to score or assist, or you can choose to take action and put the puck in the net. The role of the coach is to help you start performing at the best level possible, to get you using your mental advantage to move past your opponents and score those winning goals.

FIVE KEYS TO "WINNING THE GOLD" IN YOUR JOB SEARCH

Just as the ultimate prize for an Olympic athlete is the gold medal, the goal of your job search is to find that right job. Here are five elements that are key to your "training regimen."

Perspective

Everything starts with the way that you look at the world. You need to understand what your personal biases or slants about the world are, and be true to them, in order to make the best decisions about the direction your career can take. Peter Jensen says, "It might be nature or nurture or life experiences (that form a person); it really doesn't matter. Once you know that about yourself, you can start to make choices." We often see that those around us are "blind" to their faults, or don't truly understand how they view things. Perception is also influenced by such external factors as our friends, family, coaches, bosses and mentors. How we see ourselves, and any opportunities that may lie before us, can either be positive or negative. Perception is both external (what others think of you) and internal (what you think of yourself). Our perception ultimately influences our views and ability to take advantage of opportunity when it arrives. You need to understand clearly what is at stake and how it may impact your perception. How have you been affected by others' views of you and what you have to offer the world?

One of my clients told me that her grandfather had said he would only agree to pay for her to take a science or engineering degree program at university. Because she chose a different path, she was not supported economically — or, more importantly, emotionally. This is an example of how the perceptions of others can have an impact on us. I have had many, many discussions with clients who are at the mid-point of their careers and are very dissatisfied. When I ask them how they chose their career path in the first place, about 80 percent tell me they were externally influenced by family or teachers who told them that they would be good at a particular type of job, or that that job would be very "secure." Because these clients did not know themselves or their own personal worth very well, they wound up being influenced by others' perceptions. The needs or desires of other people in our lives are often played out even in our own career choices.

Still, external voices can be very important in helping us affirm or question how opportunities might best fit with our personality. That's why everyone should have a personal board of directors to help. This could include former supervisors, professors, colleagues or ministers. You may be surprised who will or will not be willing to be on your board. The key is to ask and to be patient; bear in mind you are not asking them to meet with you monthly, but rather in an informal, ongoing way. As you make major decisions, you want to be able to pick up the phone or e-mail them to get their take on career issues. Your board members should be secure and successful in their own way, have diverse perspectives, be wise and honest, and have a genuine interest in you. The key is to create the broadest possible perspective so you can be the very best you can be.

Imagery

Our society has strayed from valuing creativity. Our focus as a society has shifted to the logical side of our brains ("left-brain" functions), away from imagery and language, which tend to be processed on the right side of the brain. Renowned cellist Yo-Yo Ma has even called imagery "the forgotten language of our youth." In a sense, we all need to go back to kindergarten and study how to be creative again, and relearn how to play. As we reconnect with the right brain, it can have a positive impact on performance. Most blockages in a professional's life occur on the inside, not the outside, so the most effective way to communicate to yourself is through your right side of the brain. You can make full use of your imagination only when you engage all the senses and treat the things you imagine as experiences. The subconscious mind doesn't differentiate between real or imaginary experiences; it treats them all very much equally.

The principle here is that if you visualize yourself going on an interview or approaching an employer, it will have exactly the same impact as if you are right there in the boardroom. High-performing athletes do something akin to this mental exercise: a goalie will imagine many different scenarios, and practise his or her response to these scenarios, thus learning how best to perform when it counts the most. In fact, in working with Canada's Olympic team, Peter Jensen has focused squarely on where 90 percent of the action is: mental preparation. You often hear of an athlete who is performing well, but who "chokes" when he or she is needed most. In 90 percent of cases, this is related to the mental side of their game — the way they are viewing themselves and their performance. The problem isn't that they have forgotten how to run or stop a puck. It's the same with a professional who is struggling with the job interview process: mental preparation is key. Indeed, it is far more important than the ability to explain your story or to understand your history.

Peter has his athletes mentally review their own performances. With practice, an athlete can literally fine-tune his or her routine while sitting down. The more refined the routine becomes in the mind's eye, the more likely it is that an excellent outcome will occur.

Mark Tewksbury, who won two gold medals for swimming in the 1992 Summer Olympics, once sneaked into a pool four months before it was even open for the season and stood on the starting blocks

— even though the pool was empty. He spent this time imagining what it would be like to compete there, going over his race in his mind. This gave him a four-month head start over his competitors. He has spoken about how this gave him added confidence as he headed into competition. Sure, he was physically prepared, but so were all of his competitors! What put him over the top was that he had a mental advantage. All performance starts and ends in the mind: it is the mind that tells the body what to do. Therefore, you need to be mentally prepared if you truly want to be ready for your next interview.

Energy Management

Managing energy, not time, is the key to achieving high-level performance. If your energy or adrenaline levels run too high, you risk choking because you get too anxious about the outcome. This is true of athletes: consider what happened to the Ottawa Senators and Detroit Red Wings in the 2005–06 National Hockey League season. Both teams did extremely well in the regular-season schedule, but during the Stanley Cup playoffs they failed to manage their energy by reserving some for when they needed it most. As a result, both teams, although heavily favoured, were eliminated in the early rounds of the playoffs. They overperformed in the regular season and under-performed when it really mattered.

Peter Jensen notes that "arousal leads to narrow focus, and narrow focus leads to missing critical information that one needs to perform at high levels." If you get angry or upset, it will hinder your ability to perform well. If you've ever found yourself running late for an interview, you'll understand how trying to make up for those lost minutes can affect you. Your energy level will peak too early, and you may overlook things that you wanted to say or questions you wanted to ask. When you're distracted or upset, your body uses up more physical and emotional energy. Energy management is especially important when you are in a situation where you will make a first impression. If you have ever worked at a trade show or been out on a sales call with a new client, you realize how much more energy that requires compared to working with an existing client or returning for a final interview.

FOUR KEY ENERGY FACTORS

Emotional: What is your current emotional state? What state are your personal relationships in? What is your confidence level like?

Physical: Are you in good health? What did you have for breakfast— or did you have breakfast at all? Do you exercise? Do you get enough sleep?

Mental: Have you been mentally lazy? Are you feeling drained or over-stimulated?

Spiritual: What state is your soul in? Have you been true to your spiritual practices?

Take the above four factors and rate where you stand on each on a scale of 1 to 10. What is your total score? Where are you scoring low? Where are you scoring high? Pay attention to your energy levels, and bring yourself up or settle down as needed. A great way to monitor your energy level is to pay attention to your breathing. Before you head into an interview or make that call, think about your breathing and pace yourself.

Focus

When I talk with clients, I will often tell them about the bull's-eye effect as it relates to curling. The key to curling is to focus on putting the rock at the centre of the ring. You must decide what you want to do, then settle upon a strategy and actions that will move you towards this goal. In the case of the women's Olympic hockey team, their goal was, obviously, to win the gold medal. In your case, it may be to fit into a new role or do well in an interview situation. As Peter Jensen says, "Once you have a destination it is amazing what you can get, you will start to notice that everything you read or see on TV shows is [suddenly] lining up with your vision. If you decide tomorrow that you are going to go to Italy, you will start to notice all kinds of Italian things." The same truism applies if you decide you want to join the police force. This clear and specific vision will open up many doors that align with this goal. Focus will also help you to pay attention to things that will make this outcome easier.

You Still Need to Work Hard

When Peter helped the women's hockey team players attain their dreams of winning the gold medal, he helped them with all of the principles I mentioned: perspective, imagery, energy management and focus. The players were a very talented group of women, and they worked very hard for every goal and win that occurred. Similarly, you need to be talented and work very hard for every interview and career situation. Make the most of each opportunity that comes your way. Otherwise, all of the principles that apply above will not matter.

There are some essential job search skills that you can't leave home without. You need to be both researcher and promoter in your job search. You are the product that you are attempting to sell, and selling yourself is not always natural. Understanding the companies you target, including their potential strengths and problems, can help you determine how and where you can fit in. A high-yield job search requires you to carefully manage your time and tasks. It is easy to start strong and then burn out just as you are getting the right job leads. Set realistic but challenging goals and assess your day-to-day productivity truthfully. You are your job-search team's workforce *and* management. It's a tough job, but you can be successful!

JOB SEARCHES CAN FAIL DUE TO:

- low confidence
- misplaced energy and time

- lack of focus
- lack of external support
- a weak or nonexistent plan
- a poor strategy
- waiting for the market to produce results
- not knowing what you are looking for
- a current negative job situation
- emotional, physical or spiritual challenges
- lack of specific and tangible goals
- poor follow-through

When you were young, wasn't there a toy that you badly wanted to receive for your birthday? And, when you finally got it, do you remember how the novelty wore off in a day? The same is true with a job search. Initially it is exciting, but this feeling can wear off. Run with the excitement and use it to motivate yourself while you can. Use the excitement to do things that you don't enjoy doing, whether it is résumé writing, networking or what have you. Most importantly, however, use this time of excitement and hype to make a plan for the course of your job hunt. Most of us do not react well to rejection. But rejection is a reality for 99 percent of all job seekers. You *will* be rejected.

So, how will you deal with it? First, have friends and family around to encourage you. Know who you are and what your value is as an employee. Don't pin all your hopes on one job. A widespread and varied job search will eventually yield an interview that leads to a new job.

Not following a plan, or spending time on details that might be enjoyable but will not yield results, wastes time. Avoid misplacing energy; instead, follow the curriculum that has been laid out and adapt it to your current situation. If you know what your passions are, skip that section. If you understand how your past job experiences have shaped your career history, skip that section — be wise with your time! If you are currently unemployed and looking for work, you have time but need help focusing that time. In the end, it's all up to you; don't waste time wondering what to do next. When you are stuck, come back to the strategy and take the next steps. Or contact a career counsellor or coach who will guide you through the stages of your job search.

PAUL HENDERSON: STAYING TRUE TO YOURSELF EQUALS LIFELONG CAREER SUCCESS

"I started to practise my autograph in Grade 5, in anticipation of the day I would be famous in the NHL."

"Henderson has scored for Canada!" These famous words were spoken by Foster Hewitt on September 28, 1972, when, at 19:26 of the third period, Paul Henderson scored the goal of the century — the winning goal of the 1972 Summit Series between Canada and the Soviet Union.

As a young boy, Paul dreamed of playing in the National Hockey League. In anticipation of that day, he started to practise signing his autograph in Grade 5. "I wanted my autograph to be legible so that they knew who I was when I signed it." Paul knew where he was going; he needed only to figure out how to get there. For most of the next decade, through a combination of focus, hard work, talent and support from coaches and family, he overcame wonky skates and early-morning practices and laid the foundation for his hockey career. He realized his NHL dreams, breaking in with the Detroit Red Wings in 1962–63. A 1968 trade sent him to the Toronto Maple Leafs, where he played six and a half seasons before jumping to the World Hockey Association's Toronto Toros and Birmingham Bulls. He also played for the Atlanta Flames before his playing career ended in 1981.

Sometimes in life, through a convergence of circumstances and experience, we can rise to a new level and achieve remarkable things. Such was the case when Paul scored his iconic goal in the Canada–Russia series. The impact of that goal was incredible, both for the country and for Paul.

After the 1972 Summit Series, Paul struggled with his identity. For the first time since he was ten years old, he needed to find a new bull's-eye, a target on which he could focus his energy, drive and discipline. He eventually found that goal, became grounded, and now works to encourage other leaders around the country to pursue their dreams with discipline and focus.

How are *you* grounded? Is it by your identity? One thing is for sure, there will be changes in your career at some point. Getting your identity grounded is key to weathering these changes. Some people find that grounding in their faith. For others, it is in athletics, family life or other things outside of their work world. The common theme is that they are not tied into temporal elements, but rather to those of a more intrinsic value. Being grounded ensures that you will become much more mature in how you handle everything life brings your way.

Paul's new goal? "I want to finish well. I care what my wife will think about me, and what my children and my grandchildren will remember of me."

Getting Out of a Job-Search Rut

Your job-search experience is a journey. And yes, you will occasionally experience difficult stretches. Therefore, you've got to ensure that you don't run out of gas. Usually when I meet a client who decides that he or she is in a "job-search rut," I'm able to identify symptoms of burnout. If you've ever experienced this yourself, I don't need to tell you that it isn't a pleasant feeling when you're trying to function while running on empty. In a large percentage of cases, job-search burnout is avoidable if you remember that you need to keep putting gas in your engine. Here are some tips that will help you avoid job-search burnout:

Define your goals for the trip. I recommend establishing clear 30-, 60-, 90- and 120-day goals. Break these down further into weekly action items that you can manage and hold yourself to.

Talk to as many people as you can. The more people you meet, the more people there are who might be able to open doors for you.

Try something new. Don't be afraid to try out a new cover letter or a new style of approach.

Stick to your budget. Make sure that you plan your finances for your job search. Count on it taking sixty days longer than you expected to make your transition to a new job.

Rest. You need to make sure your body and mind are well rested in order to get the most out of each day.

Schedule some time for fun.

If you practise this method, no matter how difficult things get for you, you will be better equipped to deal with them. And conversely, encouraging events will become that much more enjoyable. Most of my clients find their thinking evolves over the course of their transition process; they learn to take a more positive approach to every challenge they face. I feel confident that they are empowered to deal with obstacles better the next time they find themselves in job-searching mode, and that they are setting themselves up for success.

FIVE KEYS TO DEALING WITH A LAYOFF

- Remember it isn't personal, it's just business. At first, you will experience all kinds of emotions that won't be dissimilar to dealing with the death of a loved one. Acknowledge these feelings, but keep your dealings with your employer on a professional level.
- Reach out to your friends and family. First, they are a great source of support; and second, they may know of new opportunities.
- Seek legal counsel. Meet with a lawyer and get good advice on what is a fair settlement. You probably won't end up in court, but this advice will help you protect your interests.
- Seek a career coach or outplacement firm. A majority of companies will invest in this service on your behalf as part of your settlement package.

> • Take a vacation. It may sound unusual, but if you can take a quick break for a week, you will come back refreshed and ready to move forward in your career search.

JOB-SEARCH PREPARATION

Society does not owe you joyful employment, but you do deserve it! A good job is earned, and it's the reward for a targeted, creative job search.

It's widely known that few jobs are won by answering want ads. Instead, you need to discover resources and be willing to ask for help. Look to friends and family who have recently performed successful job searches, or talk with a career coach. Don't let the negative things that people have said about you get in your way. Did a teacher say you would never succeed? Did a loved one say that you weren't suited for a type of job? Most of these comments focus on your lack of ability with a *learned* skill. Use the negative things people say to encourage you to make a change for the better. If you are a person who doesn't like meeting people or starting conversations, consider the job search a prime opportunity to get over this uneasiness.

Finding a job requires that potential employers get to know you. The job search is like a product launch or advertising campaign in which *you* are the product you're marketing. Meet with employers on a daily basis. Aim to set up at least one face-to-face meeting per day, and target a minimum of five per day by phone. If you are making contact via the Internet, you are limited only by the number of companies you can find. Five contacts a day may seem like a lot, and it is; but the more contacts you make, the faster you will rectify your current employment situation.

Your mother told you to say "please" and "thank you," and that is good advice during the search. Write thank-you notes (more about how to do this later) and extend common courtesies to every employer and person you contact during the search. You will need a support circle to sustain you during a long search. Spend time with people you like and who support you.

You'll also need to manage your emotional and physical states by getting involved in other activities, whether it's volunteering or playing a sport. These are also great ways to make contacts and find new job leads. Most communities have job- and career-support groups, so look them up and check them out. These resources may not be an ideal fit for you, but it may be helpful to have people who are facing similar struggles to encourage and motivate you.

A job search costs money and time — make sure you can afford it before you quit your job. A high-quality search is a full-time job, and you should treat it as such. Create sufficient time in your day to do it well. Think of it this way: If the average search takes about 200 hours, you can spend five weeks working full time (at forty hours per week) or spend forty weeks working five hours a week. The longer it takes, the more it will cost you. That said, don't search 24/7. Make sure you set aside time that you can spend not thinking about it.

Many people have found it useful to keep a journal. This allows you to track what you have done as well as what you *might do*. Remember that no idea is a bad idea. If you come up with a way of making contact or searching for a job that isn't contained within these pages, great! Try it out; you just may have stumbled on the newest job-search technique. (Twenty years ago, no one could have imagined posting résumés electronically on the Internet.) Spend ten minutes every day recapping what you have done, including the successes and frustrations. Eventually this will inspire you because you can see the progress you have made.

Don't settle! Over the coming weeks you will proceed through steps to understand what your right job is; when you realize what it is, don't stop until you get that job. A job search requires persistence. One of the biggest mistakes you can make is to give up too soon.

TOOLS OF THE TRADE

Just as you wouldn't play tennis without a racquet or sew without a needle and thread, you shouldn't conduct a job search without the proper equipment.

An operations centre. Convert a spare bedroom or study at home into your job-search sanctuary. If space is limited, create some on the kitchen table or on a desk, and set it aside exclusively for job-search activities. Try to do your work from the same place: half of the challenge of the job search is to make it a habit. Every time you enter your operations centre, your mind should immediately go into job-search mode. The rest of your necessary job-search equipment should be in place in your operations centre.

OPERATIONS CENTRE DOS AND DON'TS

- DO make the area private.
- DO make it pleasant by surrounding yourself with good lighting, photographs of significant people, inspirational quotes, encouraging cards and access to food and drink.
- DON'T locate it in your living room or in your easy chair in front of the television.
- DON'T spend an inordinate amount of time setting up the space; make do with what you have.

Telephone. This is the most essential piece of job-searching equipment! Make sure your voice-mail message is professional; don't use a cute message created by your kids. Keep it short. Something like: "Hi, this is the confidential voice mail of John Smith. I am currently unable to take your call, but if you leave me your name and number, I will return your call as soon as possible. You can also reach me via e-mail at johnsmith@gmail.com. Thank you." Another option is a cell phone; this allows you to be contacted at any time and anywhere, preventing you from missing phone calls from prospective employers.

Computer, printer and high-speed Internet. These are invaluable, although you can get by without them if you're near a public library or Internet café that offers these services. E-mail access and the ability to save drafts and master copies of documents all make the job-search process easier. There is a host of resources and job-search options that only exist on the Internet. As well, the Internet can be used to network and make first contact with a prospective target company. If you do not currently have a computer, it is a worthwhile investment.

An electronic organizer (also known as a PDA or personal digital assistant) will help you keep track of your appointments and contacts. Two popular brands are Palm and BlackBerry.

A briefcase gives you an air of professionalism when you attend an interview, while helping to keep you organized and allowing you to carry documents such as your résumé with you wherever you go.

Portfolios aren't just for artists. The portfolio can include examples of work you have created, performance reviews, awards and client feedback.

Business cards are inexpensive and easy to distribute. Be sure to include all of your contact information.

Professional stationery on which to print your letters and résumés will create the best impression.

Miscellaneous office supplies such as file folders, sticky notes and a stapler will come in handy.

CHAPTER FOUR

MARKETING YOU!

Your job search is akin to a product launch or an advertising campaign, except in this case *you* are the product being offered. When you think about marketing yourself, what kind of emotions does it draw out? Chances are, you'll feel some sense of anxiety, and maybe just a hint of resistance to the idea. Most professionals would prefer that employers seek *them* out, or that they get a call from a headhunter. It's understandable: we are much better at selling ideas or things we are passionate about than we are at selling ourselves. But once you get the hang of "marketing you," you will stand the best chance of getting the position you want. Think of it as the foundation upon which your career brand is built.

Two of the most important tools you will have at your disposal in this marketing campaign are your résumé and the accompanying cover letter. These items give voice to what you have to offer the market. Your experiences, skills and talents constitute a package that, presented properly, will pique the customer's attention — in this case, the customer is the hiring team or the human resources (HR) manager. To make the sale *or* get the job, you have to stand out from the other candidates.

Hiring climates change. In the early days of the website Workopolis.com, employees weren't in very great demand — it was a buyer's (or employer's) market. More recently, the balance of power in certain parts of the country is shifting in favour of the job seeker. For instance, in British Columbia, Alberta and Saskatchewan, the job market is overheated — it's a hot seller's market. Ontario, on the other hand, is currently more balanced. These fluctuations naturally have an impact on employers' flexibility. When there are more jobs than job-seekers, employers will train and move new prospects and give them all kinds of incentives to join their firm. Smart employers get creative. No matter what the climate, though, this is a two-way street: if you intend to sell yourself to an employer, you must show them what you have to offer them. You need to tell them about your most marketable talents, values and passions, as well as the areas in which you are willing to grow. Nurturing your marketing skill set will give you an advantage in any employment climate. In tight markets, it will give you an edge over other candidates; when it's a seller's market, you will be better equipped to attract top-quality options.

SEAN PRONGER: DREAM BIG AND PREPARE FOR YOUR NEXT SHIFT

"I loved playing, practising, the rink, the guys and the workouts. I was like a fan sitting on the bench in awe … everything about it, I loved."

Knowing when to leave is always the professional athlete's dilemma. Sean Pronger had played professional hockey for eleven years and created a wonderful life for his family. Still, he was well aware that an athlete's career has an expiry date, and he had often contemplated his life after hockey. As long as he still enjoyed the game, he wanted to stay in it, but one day "the fun started to fade away, inside and outside of the game." So, after a workout in 2005, he arrived at a decision while resting in his loft. "I am done," he shouted down to his wife. "That's it!"

Embarking on his post-NHL life, Sean experienced many of the common fears and doubts associated with moving on to a new career. What would he do? Would he enjoy it? Would he have to start in the mailroom? In fact, these questions illustrate why many players stay in the game even though they are past their prime: they are afraid to leave because they don't know where they will go next.

"I have only played in the NHL," was one concern that Sean raised when I worked with him to help him understand what he had to offer the job market. He needed to recognize that many of the talents that had enabled him to do well in hockey — leadership and people skills, along with sound logic and problem-solving skills — could be transferred to other fields. His other strengths were more character-related: commitment, perseverance, work ethic, adaptability and ability to function as part of a team.

One key advantage that Sean brought to the table was his network. "As a professional athlete, people want to meet you all the time." He worked diligently to leverage his relationships and meet as many people as he could in a variety of industries. Sean also understood the value of developing and projecting his confidence — he had seen the difference it had made in his game. Now, making the transition to a new career, it would be crucial for him to project this same confidence to potential employers.

Through our assessment, coaching and building a game plan, Sean was able to land a new career, one that makes use of both his sports experience and his soft skills. He joined a California-based sports development company that provides technology and tools for coaches and players to help them improve their performance. The attributes that saw him through a decade in pro hockey will carry him through the next phase of his career.

WHAT CAN YOU OFFER AN EMPLOYER?

All right, I hear you say, I need to show employers what I have to offer them. But what *do* I have to offer? Here are three areas to consider.

Know what you have to offer. Simply put, this means that you must sell what you *can do*, in addition to what you *have done*. When a successful company has a product to promote, it doesn't simply rhyme off a list of features in its advertising: it outlines the *benefits* of these features. In your job search, emphasize high-value, transferable skills, and show that you understand how a prospective employer can utilize them. This is directly related to the next point.

Understand the business's needs. If you understand what a company needs, you can make a compelling case as to why this particular company needs to hire *you* instead of anyone else. You need to demonstrate not only that you have transferable skills, but that these can be applied to your new job in order to solve the company's problems. If you follow the money, you probably will not go wrong: if you can show that you can help the business make money or save money, you will do well.

It is always about the employer. Your cover letter is a link between your résumé and the description of the job being offered. It is primarily a selling document, one whose primary purpose is to answer the question, "What's in it for me?" Employers are looking for someone who is passionate about working for them; they are also looking for evidence that you have read the job description, understood their needs and have shown your attributes address those needs.

FIVE KEYS TO MARKETING YOU

Who. Know what talents, passions, experiences and education you have to offer, and be able to express them in a very clear and concise way.

What. What is your competitive advantage? What can you do that is very distinctive within the market?

Where. Have specific examples of areas where your skills have saved or made money for the company. Outcomes matter.

Why. Have a clear picture of what the employer wants and why your background is especially well suited to the specific position they are hiring for.

How. Your résumé, interview skills, blog, references and how you present yourself are all elements that the hiring company will connect with you. Details matter!

THE RÉSUMÉ

Over a decade ago, my wife and I took a year to travel and work in Asia, teaching English for a non-governmental organization. When we returned to North America, we were confronted with the challenge of reintegrating ourselves into society — primarily, we needed jobs. The first hurdle was our calling cards: we needed new résumés. Truth be told, I've always been quite confident when it comes to understanding what I have to offer and knowing how to suitably package myself, but I never enjoyed the process of writing and condensing my life experiences in a few pages. I agonized over every detail. Did I have the right dates and correct information? What style and format should I use? In the end I commissioned my wife to pull together the document I had been struggling over. So I understand first-hand what it's like to face the challenge of writing a résumé.

And it *is* a challenge. Writing a résumé is an art; fortunately, it is a field that has been well researched. The methodology I outline here is the culmination of years of experience with résumés. If you have an old résumé, dig it out. It will provide you with a good starting point, but you'll need to create a new one that will get you past the initial scanning process and into the interview.

A common problem shared by many job searchers is that they don't know what potential employers do with a résumé when they receive it. We like to think that the administrative assistant opens our carefully sealed and chosen envelope with great anticipation, and behold our fine paper and painstakingly chosen font with awe that most people reserve for the first time they catch sight of the Sistine Chapel. Unfortunately, when someone receives hundreds of résumés, each envelope is torn open in haste, the résumé scanned for keywords and tossed onto one of three piles: definitely interview, maybe interview, definitely not.

A recent survey of 5,000 Canadian and American recruiters found that 63 percent of job seekers send unsolicited résumés, 34 percent fail to adhere to the specific résumé posting instructions and a whopping 71 percent send résumés that don't even match the posted job description. Assuming you don't make these mistakes, you still have important things to consider when creating your résumé. Is it visually appealing? Does it catch the employer's eye? Can they find your information quickly and easily? Do they understand why they're looking at it? Are you a suitable applicant for the position? All of these questions are asked and decided upon in a matter of seconds — if you're lucky, a minute or two.

That said, I don't want you to be discouraged. Your résumé is a key part of your marketing plan and a crucial tool in your journey to the next job. It showcases the attributes that tell your potential employer you are worth considering. Be clear about one thing: a résumé does not get you a job, but it *can* get you to the interview stage. Think of it as the advertisement that attracts the customer into the store: you may be the most qualified person for the job, but if your résumé doesn't entice the employer to want to find out more about you, you won't get the interview, let alone the job. I want you to maximize every opportunity you get. If you take the time to prepare a targeted résumé and develop a strategic approach, you'll get results. I know this because I see it happen constantly. So, how does your résumé stack up? How, in the fifteen seconds or so in which you have the screeners' attention, do you convince them to put your résumé into the "definitely interview" pile?

The latest and newest challenge in résumé writing is how to beat the computer. The majority of large and midsize companies have resorted to a computer-based initial scan of the résumé. These systems look for specific keywords. If you are missing those words, you are excluded, even if your experience makes you the best and most qualified candidate. Is it fair? No. But it *is* reality. So how can you incorporate all those aspects into a résumé?

You must be honest. This is key. If you lie, you will eventually get caught. Employers expect you to put your best foot forward, but make sure you're still being truthful.

It is your job to sell yourself. If you have trouble talking about your achievements, think about ways other people — whether they are friends or former employers — have described you. What would your biggest fan or favourite co-worker say about your top qualities?

A résumé is about your future as well as your past. A résumé doesn't exist solely as a report on your past: it is also designed to help you create a new future. Write your résumé with an eye towards where you want to be: the insights you have gained with respect to values, talents and dreams all need to fit in your résumé — particularly those that relate directly to the job you are pursuing.

A résumé is for the reader. Before crafting your résumé, think about it from the employers point of view. How can you arrange the information to highlight what the employer is looking for? Are the skills, experience and values they seek front and centre?

The Seven Deadly Sins of Résumé Writing

Before you proceed, study your résumé, being especially alert for these pitfalls.

Lack of professionalism. Human resources staff are busy, so respect their needs. Don't be clever and use puns or cute phrases. Your résumé must look professional.

Carelessness. If you are sloppy with spelling or dates, or you forget to attach page two, you send the message that you could be just as careless on the job. There is no room for errors.

Vagueness or non-related jargon. The people receiving your résumé need to understand what you are writing. Don't write that you were the "asst VP of mpr"; spell out your title in full. If the information is worth including, it is worth taking the time to help the reader understand it.

Misrepresentation. Just as you shouldn't lie, you shouldn't embellish or include comments that are in poor taste.

Overkill and underkill. You might have been the "greatest software designer in the world," but if you didn't win an award, it will suffice to call yourself a "skilled or competent software designer."

Too much personal information. Stick to the basics — leave out your age, height and weight, along with information on your health and family. It is great that you are happily married, but your potential employer probably doesn't care.

Verbosity. Too many words make the reader work too hard. Be concise. Edit.

Types of Résumés

All jobs are not created equal, and neither are all résumés. Different situations call for different styles. There are three types: chronological, functional, and a combination of the two. The following tips and examples will help you choose the type that best suits your needs.

Chronological Résumé

In this type of résumé, your job history is organized chronologically, with the most recent information first. Job titles and organizations are emphasized, and duties and accomplishments are described in detail. A chronological résumé is easy to read, since it highlights the names of employers and job titles and emphasizes career growth. This type is best suited to those whose career goals are clear and whose objectives are aligned with their work history. Chronological résumés are useful in situations that have some or all of the following characteristics:

- your recent employers and/or job titles are impressive
- you are staying in the same career field

- your job history shows progress
- you are working in a field where traditional job-search methods are utilized (such as education or the government)

Chronological résumés can be troublesome if your current job-search situation fits one of the following descriptions:

- you are changing careers
- you have changed employers frequently
- you want to de-emphasize your age
- you have been absent from the job market, or there are large gaps in your employment history

(Contact information — indicate how the employer can reach you)

NAME
Address
City, Province Postal Code
Phone number • E-mail address

(Use a professional title to show what types of markets you have worked in or wish to work in)

Senior Management Professional
BUSINESS DEVELOPMENT / MARKETING / TECHNOLOGY
High-Growth Companies

PROFESSIONAL EXPERIENCE:

(Work history — list the companies you worked for, positions you held, dates of employment, a sentence or two describing your responsibilities and three or four bullets highlighting your accomplishments)

Company #1, City, Province
Position Held   **Dates you worked**
Responsibilities included managing and executing annual national trade show involving six cities across the U.S.; strengthening contractor relationships; enhancing vendor relationships with customers and maximizing efficiencies and improvements through program logistics and cost-savings opportunities.
- Improved trade show attendance by 10 percent while cutting annual expenses by 25 percent, allowing an increase in the number of cities in 2004 from two to six

Company #2, City, Province
Position Held   **Dates you worked**
Responsibilities included...
  • Achievements

Company #3, City, Province
Position Held   **Dates you worked**
Responsibilities included...
  • Achievements

EDUCATION AND TRAINING:

(List the colleges / universities you attended, the degrees you attained and any special awards and honours you earned)

B.A. (Psychology): University, City, Province   Date
Certification: ABC Company, City, Province   Date
Executive Management Workshops: University, City, Province   Date

ASSOCIATIONS AND AFFILIATIONS:

Board Member: City Downtown Development Committee,
City, Province   Date
Board Member: City Chamber of Commerce, City, Province   Date

AWARDS:

Best Exhibit and Best Presentation in Consumer Trade Shows
in New Brunswick   Date

TECHNICAL SKILLS:

(Include skills related to the position / career field that you are applying for; e.g., computer skills, language skills)

Software:
Microsoft Office (Outlook, Word, Excel, PowerPoint)
Windows 9x, 2000, XP
Design / Copy Writing / Programming Special Features /
Integrating E-Commerce capabilities

Functional Résumé

In a functional résumé, skills and accomplishments developed through work, academic and community experiences are highlighted. Your skills and potential can be stressed and lack of experience or possible gaps in work history de-emphasized. It is important to realize that employers often view functional résumés more critically for these very same reasons. The functional résumé is advantageous when:

- you want to emphasize capabilities not used in recent work experience
- you want to emphasize personal qualities relevant to the job, such as industriousness, a co-operative attitude or related interests and aptitudes
- you want to focus on capabilities rather than a lengthy employment history
- your career growth has not been continuous and progressive
- you have a variety of unrelated work experiences
- your work has involved freelancing or consulting or has been temporary in nature

The functional résumé is not advantageous when:

- you have little work experience
- you want to emphasize promotions and career growth
- you are working in highly traditional fields, such as teaching, accounting or politics, where employers should be highlighted

(Contact information — indicate how the employer can reach you)

NAME
Address
City, Province Postal Code
Phone number • E-mail address

(Use a professional title to show what types of markets you have worked in or wish to work in)

Senior Management Professional
BUSINESS DEVELOPMENT / MARKETING / TECHNOLOGY
High-Growth Companies

(Begin with highlights and qualifications — a customized section of your résumé that lists key achievements, skills, traits and experience relevant to the position you are applying for. This highlights your relevant experience and lets the prospective employer know that you have taken the time to create a résumé that shows how you are qualified for the job.)

Dynamic Senior Business Development Leader with 20+ years' experience spearheading successful ventures throughout global business markets. Expert strategist, analyst, planner, team leader, negotiator and business driver who has delivered dramatic gains in revenues, profits and market share. Proven track record combines expertise in strategic market planning, organizational leadership and project management with strong qualifications in campaign design, new product / service development and market launch.

(Include a table to list the key skills that are relevant to the job you are applying for, based on what you have done in the past)

- Strategic Planning and Business Development
- Marketing and Business Development
- New Venture Start-Up and Management
- Field and Corporate Sales Leadership
- Critical Problem-Solving and Analysis

- Executive–Client Relationship Management
- Cross-Functional Team Building
- Product Design and Development
- Profit and Loss Performance
- Multi-Channel Sales and Distribution

**Delivering Leadership Strategies,
Driving Revenue and Profit Growth**

PROFESSIONAL EXPERIENCE:

(Work history — list the companies you worked for, positions you held, dates of employment, a sentence or two describing your responsibilities and three or four bullets highlighting your accomplishments)

Company #1, City, Province
Position Held   **Dates you worked**
Responsibilities included managing and executing annual national trade show involving six cities across the U.S.; strengthening contractor relationships; enhancing vendor relationships with customers and maximizing efficiencies and improvements through program logistics and cost-savings opportunities.
  • Improved trade show attendance by 10 percent while cutting annual expenses by 25 percent, allowing an increase in the number of cities in 2004 from two to six

Company #2, City, Province
Position Held   **Dates you worked**
Responsibilities included...
  • Achievements

Company Name #3, City, Province
Position Held   **Dates you worked**
Responsibilities included...
  • Achievements

EDUCATION AND TRAINING:

(List the colleges / universities you attended, the degrees you attained and any special awards and honours you earned)

B.A. (Psychology): University, City, Province   Date

Certification: ABC Company, City, Province   Date

Executive Management Workshops: University, City, Province   Date

ASSOCIATIONS AND AFFILIATIONS:

Board Member: City Downtown Development Committee,
City, Province   Date

Board Member: City Chamber of Commerce, City, Province   Date

AWARDS:

Best Exhibit and Best Presentation in Consumer Trade Shows
in New Brunswick   Date

TECHNICAL SKILLS:

*(Include skills related to the position / career field that you are applying
for; e.g., computer skills, language skills)*

Software:
Microsoft Office (Outlook, Word, Excel, PowerPoint)
Windows 9x, 2000, XP
Design / Copy Writing / Programming Special Features /
Integrating E-Commerce capabilities

Combination Résumé

This format combines the best elements of the chronological and the functional. It presents patterns of accomplishments and skills in "Areas of Effectiveness" or "Qualifications Summary" sections. It also includes a brief work history and education summary. This format is advantageous for those who wish to change to a job in a related career field. If you have had no luck getting past the screening process with a chronological résumé, the combination may get you to the interview stage. These are some of the advantages of a combination résumé:

- It allows you to establish early on what you have accomplished in your career and what skills and attributes you can offer.
- It provides a work history to diffuse the suspicions that a functional résumé sometimes arouses.

The "Scannable" Résumé

As employers turn to optical scanning of résumés — and storing the results in electronic databases from which they can be quickly retrieved when looking for suitable candidates — many job seekers design one résumé for human eyes and another for electronic scanning.

The same rules apply when writing a scannable résumé. Your résumé is a place to express individuality and style. However, some font and style choices could present too much of a challenge for the scanner. If you follow the tips below, the system will be better able to extract your information accurately. Also, these systems search for applicants by using keywords or phrases. In order for your résumé to have appeal in your chosen career field, use the language of the field. While sections that highlight experience, education, languages, technical skills and other categories are important, emphasize specific skills and achievements.

TIPS FOR CREATING A SCANNABLE RÉSUMÉ

- Use white or light-coloured paper.
- Use 8.5-by-11-inch paper.
- Use fairly plain fonts such as Futura, Times New Roman or Courier. Avoid ornate fonts and fonts where the characters touch.
- Use a font size between 10 and 14 points.
- Don't use italics or underlining; these may cause problems for the scanner.
- Use **boldface** for emphasis.
- Use vertical and horizontal lines sparingly. Leave at least a quarter of an inch of space around the line.
- Avoid graphics, boxes, shading or shadowing.
- Submit an original printed by a laser printer. Print on only one side of the paper.
- Don't fold or staple, as the résumé will not scan well.
- Describe your accomplishments using the language of your desired profession to ensure that the résumé will be filed according to your skills. Look at the keywords that the target company uses on its website; if there are other openings posted, analyze the language *they* use.
- At the same time, be concise and use words that will describe your skills accurately and quickly.

- Don't compress or expand the space between letters or lines. Don't double-space within sections.
- Display your name at the top, with your address and phone number on the next line directly beneath. Each phone number should be listed on its own line.
- Avoid a two-column format.
- Don't lie or embellish.
- Don't feel that you have to limit yourself to one page.
- Use common headings such as "Objective," "Employment History" and "Education."
- Be specific.

When posting your résumé to online databases, remember these five points:

- **Plain text.** The absence of formatting makes it easier for you to post within the job site and to adjust the layout and margins to match the site's format.
- **Keywords.** Internal recruiters will search the database for keywords; make sure the keywords from the description of the job you're after are in your résumé.
- **Length.** Keep your lines to a maximum of 65 characters; this makes it easier for recruiters to read and keeps your information tight and engaging.
- **Simplicity.** Be careful with bullets, lines, etc. Most online databases will have trouble aligning these special characters; use CAPS to emphasize points.
- **Double-checking.** Before you press "enter," you would do well to have someone else double-check the information; once you press "send" you will no longer be able to control the first impression you make.

The next exercise, My Master Résumé Data Sheet, will help you consolidate the basics you need to design or redesign your résumé. Remember to list all experiences that may be useful, not just those that are specific to one job.

MY MASTER RÉSUMÉ DATA SHEET
Name:
Local address:
Permanent address:
Phone number:
E-mail address:
Web page (if appropriate):
Current work objectives (if applicable):
Special skills and experiences:
Personal mission statement:
Education:
Work experience:
Employer:
Length of employment:
Position:
Accomplishments:
Samples of best work, if relevant:
Volunteer work, community involvement, association membership:
Publications, reports, presentations, awards:
Activities and interests:

When you are writing a job-specific résumé, sequence the categories according to what is most important to the employer and to meeting your career objective. A recent college graduate with limited experience may want to showcase education first, as it is their most significant and recent achievement. Education should also be listed first when, as in the case of teaching, law, medicine or engineering, it is a qualifying requirement. In a situation where an applicant wants to emphasize significant work or extracurricular experience, or when an employer seeks to fill jobs in areas such as sales, public relations or merchandising, the experience or work history category may be listed first.

The Parts of a Résumé
Contact Information

- Put your name, capitalized and in bold type, on the top line.
- On the lines below your name, list your street address, city, province or state and postal or zip code.
- Include phone number(s) where you can be reached. Designate your home phone with an "H," your work number, if applicable, with a "W," and a cell number, if applicable, with a "C." **Warning:** if you are still employed and you include your work number on the résumé, phone calls may raise questions with your current employer. A good rule is to include your work number only if you are not worried about your current employer finding out about your job search.

Career/Job Objective

The purpose of the objective statement is to inform the reader of your career goals and qualifications. If your search has a variety of objectives, you may want to relay the most relevant one to the job posting you are applying for in the accompanying cover letter. Your opening statement or career/job objective informs the employer that you are accomplished, focused and have a proven track record. An effective career/job objective highlights:

- the type and/or level of position you are seeking
- the work environment you are seeking (that is, the type and style of organization)
- your skills and qualifications

Before you rush to define your career/job objective, it is important to understand the pros and cons of including one on your résumé. The pros: it identifies your specific interests and where you would fit in the organization, and presents the impression of a focused, self-confident person. The cons: it may be too broad and meaningless, which reflects indecision, and it may be too exclusive, eliminating you from a job you might consider or be considered for. Never include an objective when you intend to use one résumé for a variety of job openings.

Qualifications or Experience Summary

An extensive background emphasizing experiences and accomplishments can be summarized in a few powerful lines. The qualifications summary is accomplishment-oriented. It is appropriate for someone with substantial experience, for someone who is changing careers and wants to demonstrate transferable skills or for someone with an eclectic background. The summary can be approached in one of two ways: as a condensed description of your career background or as a tool to generally describe your skills and attributes.

Education

- Start with your most recent degree or the program in which you are currently enrolled. List other degrees or relevant education credentials in reverse chronological order.
- Highlight your degree by using **bold type**, CAPITAL LETTERS or <u>underlining</u>.
- If the degree is relevant to your job objective, begin with degree and major, followed by university, location of university, and date of graduation or anticipated date of graduation.
- If the degree is not directly related to your current job objective, begin with university, followed by location, degree and major, and graduation date.
- If you are within two semesters of graduation, do not use "expected or anticipated" with month/year of graduation.
- If you have a high grade point average (GPA) or have graduated First Class Standing, include this information. You may

chose to highlight your GPA on a new line, or in an educational highlights section. Note: some employers believe that the absence of a GPA indicates an extremely poor score.

- If your education relates to your objective and has been completed within the past three years, it should be listed in the first section. If not, it should follow the work experience section.

Educational Highlights

This section is most effective when you have impressive educational experience — coursework, research or special knowledge — directly related to your objective. Adding this section is useful when you have developed skills and specific knowledge through your education rather than work experience.

- Consider listing relevant coursework under the appropriate degree.
- An alternative to highlighting courses is to list the skills and knowledge acquired through important courses and research.

Employment Experience (Chronological Résumé)

- Begin with your current or most recent position, and work backwards, chronologically. Devote more space to recent employment.
- If your job titles relate to your current job objective, start each position description with job titles. If not, begin with the company name.
- Follow job title and organizational information with the company's city and province. Use the first and last month and year to describe dates of employment.
- Describe the last three to five positions in detail. Summarize earlier positions unless relevant to your objective.
- Do not show every position change with each employer. List only the most recent position and describe promotions.
- Do not repeat skills that are common to several positions.
- Within each listed position, stress the major accomplishments and responsibilities that demonstrate your competency. It is

not necessary to include all responsibilities, as they will be assumed by employers.

- Tailor your position descriptions to future job or career objectives.
- Use a one-page résumé for entry-level positions. Two-page résumés are acceptable as long as the information on both pages demonstrates the skills and/or experiences relevant to your chosen profession.

Employment Experience (Functional Résumé)

- Use two to four sentences to summarize each area of skill or experience.
- Develop the skills heading based on the areas you want to emphasize to employers and/or those that are most related to your job objective.
- Describe your skills in short phrases and place under the appropriate categories.
- Rank the phrases within each category and place the most important skill or accomplishment first.
- Do not identify employers within the skills sections.
- List a brief history of your work experience at the bottom, giving job title, employer and dates. If you have had no work experience or a very spotty work record, leave out the employment section entirely.

Other Résumé Points
Overall Résumé Tips

- Do not use "Résumé" in the heading on page one. This is obvious.
- Include the page number at the top of each subsequent page.
- Put your name at the top of each subsequent page.
- Start phrases with action verbs such as led, designed, initiated or scheduled. If you worked as a team member, use phrases such as "in collaboration with," etc.

- Do not use passive verbs such as assisted, helped, participated.
- Do not repeat information.
- Do not create a new section with only one bullet of text under it. If the bullet of information is important, make it fit into a different section.
- Proofread your draft and have a competent friend or family member review it.

Résumé Proofreading

Have you ever seen a résumé that had spelling or grammatical errors? The mistake, even though it sticks out like a sore thumb, may not seem like a major blunder to you, but potential employers perceive these errors as a sign of lack of attention to detail. A hiring manager could pass you over because of such a simple résumé faux pas.

Punctuation

- Include periods at the end of full sentences.
- Avoid the use of exclamation marks.
- Be consistent in your use of punctuation.

Spelling

- Don't use words you aren't familiar with.
- Keep a dictionary beside you while you write, and refer to it often.
- Perform a computer spell check, but remember that a spell checker won't pick up on some errors — for instance, it won't know the difference between "to" and "too" or "then" and "than."

Other Points

- Capitalize every proper noun.
- Abbreviate province or state names correctly. For example, Ontario should be abbreviated as ON.
- Check your dates. Incorrect employment dates could cost you a job.
- Ensure your date formats are consistent.
- If beginning a sentence with a number, write it out (nine vs. 9).

- Ensure that your contact information is relevant and current.
- Use the same line-spacing style throughout the entire résumé.

Tips to Improve Your Proofreading Accuracy

- Relax. You're more likely to miss things if you're stressed or tired.
- Place a business card or piece of paper under the line of text you're proofreading. This will help to keep you focused and prevent you from being distracted by the next line.
- Read out loud. Your ears will often pick up on problems that your eyes don't spot on the page.
- Check spelling of difficult words by reading them backwards, right to left. This will force you to focus.
- After proofreading your résumé, set it aside for a period of time. You'll come back with a fresh perspective and will be more likely to find mistakes.
- Give yourself enough time to proofread thoroughly. Take time to polish your résumé.
- Have a friend or family member proofread your résumé as well. You'll be surprised by what a fresh pair of eyes can find.

Use the Résumé Checklist below and on the next three pages to ensure that you have remembered everything.

RÉSUMÉ CHECKLIST

Overall Appearance

- Looks professional
- Is interesting and inviting to read
- Language is easy to read and understand

Layout

- Highlights my strongest qualifications or credentials
- Uses headings to help establish common ground with employer

(e.g., graduate business education, professional social work, training, retail experience)

- Separates sections and incorporates enough white space for easy reading
- Uses **bold type,** <u>underlining</u>, different type styles and sizes to emphasize keywords
- Has margins wide enough for easy reading
- Is one or two pages in length

Printing and Reproduction

- Paper is high-quality heavyweight bond
- Paper is off-white, ivory, light tan, light grey, or another conservative and conventional colour
- Reproduction is clear, clean and professional
- Print is letter-quality, never photocopied

Content

- Demonstrates the ability to do the job and speaks to employer's needs
- Supports and substantiates objectives
- Stresses transferable professional skills, accomplishments and results
- Contains personal data relevant to my objective (e.g., language skills, computer skills)
- Omits racial, religious or political affiliations unless a bona fide occupational qualification

Language

- Expresses thoughts succinctly
- Uses short, action-oriented phrases rather than complete sentences
- Begins phrases with action verbs
- Uses active rather than passive voice

- Is free of grammatical, spelling or punctuation errors
- Uses vocabulary of working world

Contact Information

- Is clearly presented at the top of page one
- Emphasizes name with capital letters and bold type
- Includes permanent and (if applicable) temporary address information
- Includes daytime and evening telephone number(s)
- Includes e-mail address

Objective (optional — use if your objective is specific)

- Includes type and level of position sought
- Describes type and size of company sought
- Emphasizes strongest qualifications and skills pertinent to desired job

Summary Statement

- Lists, in a few lines, qualifications and accomplishments

Education

- Most recent degree or program in; date of graduation or anticipated date
- List of other degrees or relevant higher education, training certificate programs, licences or short courses
- Name and location of university, college or training institution
- Major or minor specialty and/or area(s) of concentration or interest
- Relevant coursework, skills or knowledge acquired through research or projects
- GPA, honours and awards

Employment Experience

- Each relevant paid, volunteer, extracurricular, intern or co-op experience listed includes: title held, organization name, city, province/state and/or country location, and dates position held
- Each position description stresses transferable skills, previous accomplishments and effectiveness (rather than a mere summary of past duties and responsibilities)
- Includes specific examples of successes and results supporting objective
- Includes examples that quantify results or successes (e.g., increased sales by $50,000, reduced turnover by 25 percent)

Affiliations and Associations (optional)

- Lists the most impressive offices held, including title and organization
- Mentions leadership roles held and transferable skills gained
- Includes pertinent professional memberships

THE COVER LETTER

First impressions are lasting — they count! And the cover letter is usually the first thing the person who screens your résumé looks at. You can influence the way the reader views your résumé by directing them to the highlights while avoiding your weak areas. You can also use the cover letter to explain gaps or challenges in your work history. A cover letter must be well researched, so do your homework and be in a position to demonstrate knowledge about the company and the industry you are targeting.

Writer's block can put the brakes to the cover letter preparation process. If you're struggling with this task, you may not be ready for it yet. However, consider the following questions. Once you have answered each one you'll be in a much better position to write an effective letter.

Why are you writing the cover letter? This may seem like a very obvious question, but you'd be surprised how many people can't answer it. What are your objectives for the cover letter? Are you hoping for an interview? Are you hoping for a short phone call? When you understand why you're writing your letter, you'll shape your ideas accordingly.

What does the company or hiring manager need? Do you understand what you're applying for? Do you know what requirements the company has? Make a short list of what the potential employer is looking for. This will help you tailor your letter and résumé so that they will be applicable to the employer's needs.

Why would the company want to hear from you? What skills or experience do you bring that the organization needs? Many people believe that they should list an inventory of all of their skills and abilities and expect the hiring manager to sift through them for the ones the company is seeking — not a great approach! Analyze the list you made from the previous question and note the corresponding skills and abilities that address these points.

Do you have any achievements that the company should know about? Write down two to four work achievements or accomplishments that relate to the position you're applying for. This will back up the claims you have made about your skills and demonstrate that you're a suitable applicant. The easier you make it for the employer to see why you're a good candidate, the more likely they are to give you a call.

Why are you interested in this company/organization? Have you researched it? If in the course of doing your research you find out that the company culture and business dealings aren't a good match for you, you probably wouldn't want to work there. On the other hand, if your research indicates that you and the organization would be a good fit, be sure to demonstrate interest and enthusiasm in your letter.

But make sure anything you say about the company is accurate. Some hiring managers choose candidates to interview based on the cover letter, and careless mistakes can put a halt to your hard work and your dreams.

DOS AND DON'TS OF COVER LETTERS

- DON'T copy your résumé verbatim. Your cover letter is an opportunity to tell your story and to explain why you would be a valuable asset to the organization. It should motivate the hiring manager to read your résumé, not bore them by making them read the exact same thing twice.
- DO begin your cover letter with the name of a person involved in the hiring process. DO NOT begin with "Dear Sir," "Dear Madam" or "To Whom It May Concern." Your best bet is to address the cover letter to the person who you want to read it. If you can't find out who that is, try "Dear Hiring Manager" or "Dear Employer."
- DON'T appear self-centred. Your cover letter isn't an autobiography. You should focus on how you can meet the employer's needs, and how you can be valuable to their organization. Limit your use of the word "I," especially at the beginning of sentences.
- DON'T sell yourself short. Your cover letter is an opportunity for you to sell yourself as a credible candidate. It should be compelling and outline the main reasons why the recipient should call you for an interview. Emphasize your top achievements!
- DON'T use a shotgun approach. If you're applying for more than one position, you can't use the same cover letter for each one. You've got to customize your letter so that it clearly shows how you'll meet the specific needs of each position and each employer.
- DON'T end on a passive note. Instead of asking the hiring manager to contact you if they're interested, make a promise to follow up. You can say something like this: "I will follow up with you in a few days to answer any initial questions that you may have. In the meantime I can be reached at (555) 555-5555."

- DO say thank you! Always thank the reader for the time spent considering your application.
- DON'T be impersonal. If you've hand-delivered or mailed your cover letter and résumé, don't forget to sign it. (If you've sent it by e-mail, a signature isn't necessary.)
- DO check for spelling errors. Have a friend proofread your letter. Spelling errors are some of the most obvious and costly mistakes that you can make.
- DON'T write the letter and let it sit for days or weeks. Write it and send it the same day.

The correct format for the name and address of the recipient is: Put the person's full name (if you know it) on line 1. On line 2, add the person's title. Put the department on line 3, the company name on line 4 and its street address on line 5. On line 6, place the city, the province or state, and the postal or zip code.

The salutation is the first thing the screener will read. Use their first name only if you have been introduced to them in that fashion. Otherwise, use Ms., Mr. or Dr. instead. Don't use Miss or Mrs., as Ms. is today's business standard.

It is ideal if you can learn the name of the person to whom you are sending the cover letter. This is not always easy, especially if you are responding to an ad posted on the Internet or in a newspaper. Don't let this discourage you from getting the right name: call the company and talk to a receptionist — or even better, to an employee in the appropriate department. Inform them that you want to address your letter and would appreciate the correct name, including the spelling and the person's title. Be gracious, and you'll be surprised at how well you do! And remember, *do not* make a spelling mistake here.

The opening paragraph of your letter needs to give the reader a reason to read on. What is the purpose of your letter? State it here in way that will hook them and encourage them to continue. If you use another person's name to connect you to the reader, make sure that the connection is legitimate. Include only a name that is recognized and respected by the reader — and make sure you have asked permission from the person you are mentioning. You also need to demonstrate knowledge of the company in the first paragraph, so work in a fact or observation that isn't common knowledge or that makes an interesting connection.

In the remainder of the body, include information about your current situation (work-wise), what you are looking for, and why the position is interesting at this point in your career. Expand on a few points from your résumé, explain any glaring gaps and tell the reader about the qualities you will bring to the job. Answer the following:

- Why are you interested in this company?
- Why are you interested in this position?
- Why, at this point in your life, are you pursuing this opportunity?

The inclusion of a statement on how you are qualified is vital. This must include keywords about your talents that directly relate to the job you are applying for.

To close a cover letter, be direct and state an action. For example, "Thank you for your consideration of my application. I will contact your office in the next ten days to see if you require any additional information regarding my qualifications." By calling back, you can provide additional information about your references, university transcripts, and so forth. You will also be able to inquire about the status of your application. In closing, "Sincerely," "Sincerely yours," "Yours truly," "Regards" or "Cordially" are all fine.

The Cover Letter Step-by-Step
Step 1: Research

- If a job description is available, read it a few times and highlight important points.
- Research the company by reading news articles, searching the Internet and making direct contact with current employees.

- Make notes of what you have learned.
- Obtain the name of the person who will receive your job application.

Step 2: Show How You Fit into the Job

- Write down the talents, passions and values that related directly or indirectly to the research you gathered from the Right Job Checklist (p. 12).
- Highlight what makes you stand out from other applicants.
- Write down the reason why the employer will be better off having you on board.
- List education and work experiences that relate to the job.

Step 3: Shape the Paragraphs

- Group or cluster points together by themes.
- Prioritize the themes (using the job description and your knowledge of the company as a touchstone).

Step 4: Write the First Draft

- Use complete sentences.
- Make important statements and create links between them, helping them flow into a clear, concise paragraph.
- Close the letter with a strong statement that will inspire the reader to contact you.

Step 5: Check the Final Copy

- Edit and re-read your work.
- Enlist a friend or colleague to read the letter and give feedback on spelling, flow and clarity.

Although you know yourself, the employer doesn't know you. You must use the cover letter to tell the potential employer about yourself. If you don't give them anything to go on, they won't be interested enough to proceed to the interview stage. In summary, a cover letter is your ticket to the interview. The letter should be no more than one page in length and consist of three to four short paragraphs. It will address the following questions:

- How did you learn about the job?
- Why are you are interested in the job?
- How you are qualified for the job?
- What steps will you take to be considered for the job?

You need to demonstrate in your cover letter how you qualify for each skill or responsibility listed in the job posting. To help you build the cover letter, use the worksheet below. In the left-hand column, write down all the skills and requirements requested in the job posting; in the right-hand column, note how your qualifications match that request. By completing this exercise, you will have the foundation for a quality letter.

COVER LETTER WORKSHEET	
Position and Skills Requirements	My Qualifications

Now use the following cover letter template and the information you have gathered using the Cover Letter Worksheet to write your letter.

Name
Address
City, Province Postal Code
Phone Number ● E-mail

Month Date, Year

Contact Person
Title
Company
Street
City, Province Postal Code

Dear Mr./Ms./Last Name:

Building company value by *(fill in one area you would like here)* is my area of expertise.

I take pleasure in providing solutions because analysis and problem-solving are innate to my character. For example, I have...

I am confident that my abilities would be a great asset to your company. I have proven myself at:

● *Copy and paste some bullets from your résumé*

These achievements are indicative of the quality and calibre of my professional career.

I am flexible to respond to the constantly changing demands in... I have overcome past challenges by...

In addition, I bring excellent communication and presentation skills, work ethic, drive and potential as evidenced early on in my career through...

I am currently exploring new positions where I can combine my expertise, experience and education to provide measurable value for your company. As such, I would be delighted to meet with you to discuss opportunities with your organization. I will phone you next week to follow up and answer any questions. I appreciate your time and consideration.

Sincerely,

REFERENCES

References serve as a reality check for the entire job-search process. Employers use them to verify what you have said about yourself, so it is imperative that they be accurate and current. Most people forget about their references until they are sitting in an interview and get asked about them. Don't be put on the spot: maintain good relations with your references; if you've lost touch with any of them, get on the phone.

The other benefit of keeping in touch with references and informing them that you are searching for a job is that they may be able to give you a lead on a job somewhere down the road.

Your references should be able to talk about your accomplishments and achievements. You want them to be able to speak about you in a way that demonstrates the value you can bring to an organization. A reference can have a greater impact when they can cite specific examples, so it's best to include people who know you in a career sense. Your references should also be at a management or professional level, because if they're recognized as leaders or key players in a company, their words will carry more weight and help you the most.

Don't use family members as references. Your references will be asked questions about you and the manner in which you work. The hiring manager is ultimately trying to find out if you are going to be a good worker, if you can solve problems and if you'll be a good fit for the organization.

Your references will be asked about specific accomplishments that you have described to the company in your interview or in your résumé, so think about people who can back up your claims. They will typically be asked about your communication skills; your ability to deal with rejection; your achievements, strengths and weaknesses; your ability to work independently or as part of a team; whether they feel you would be a good fit for the job in question and whether they would either hire you or work with you again.

To prepare your references, give them key pieces of information. Let them know about the job that you've applied for and that you've used them as a reference, send them a copy of your current résumé and confirm that their contact information is current. Although reference checks come later in the job-search process, take some time right now to ensure you're prepared.

Do not include phrases such as "references available upon request" in your résumé or cover letter. You should have references available, as your future employer will require them further on in the hiring process. A good reference can influence the hiring manager's final decision. Both professional and peer references may be useful. Identify three of each.

Make sure that you thank your references for providing this service for you; follow this up with a short note. The Master Reference List below is designed to consolidate your reference information. The Reference List for Potential Employers that follows should be completed prior to every job interview, because it will instantly provide the employer with a complete list of your references.

MASTER REFERENCE LIST					
Name	Title	Company	Phone	E-mail	Notes

REFERENCE LIST FOR POTENTIAL EMPLOYERS
Reference List for: (your name here)
Address:
Phone Number:
Name:
Position/Company:
Phone:
E-mail:
Best Time to Contact Them:
Personal or Professional Reference:

Written References

A written reference should be limited to one page. Any longer and the reader may not read it as carefully as you would like. What should a written reference accomplish? Ideally, the reference letter will paint a picture of your tangible skills and give specific examples of them, as well as offer a general sense of such intangibles as your attitude, work ethic, ability to respond to challenges and to work as a team member.

Who Should Be a Reference?

I'm often asked whether non-work-related references, such as a reference from a longtime friend, are worth including. I don't recommend that you use your best friend, but someone from a volunteer organization can be very useful. This person can attest to things that will make your potential employer feel good about you as a part of their company. Another non-work reference that is useful, especially if your experience is limited and/or you are a recent graduate, is a university professor. There is a level of respect associated with professors that will add legitimacy to your application.

For a work reference, how far back should you go? This depends on the number of jobs you have had and the length of time you spent with your last employer. I wouldn't suggest that you go back more than five years unless the reference can attest to a skill or accomplishment that is directly and strongly applicable to the job you are applying for.

It is good to have a wide range of references you can call upon when applying for various jobs. That said, you do not need to obtain references from all of your previous employers. If you have lost touch with your former boss or he or she has left the company, don't worry about not including them.

THANK-YOU LETTERS

After every interaction with a potential employer, specifically after interviews, you need to send a thank-you card or note. Not only is this thoughtful, but it brings you back into the interviewer's mind. The thank-you note allows you one last opportunity to reinforce your suitability for the job. It may take the form of a card or formal letter.

I strongly recommend thank-you letters. A letter can have a tremendous impact on the decision-making process and your ultimate success. If you aren't already sending them out, start doing so after your next interview.

These days, it's a valid question whether you should send a handwritten note or an e-mail message. The answer depends on a few things. How did the company get in touch with you? If they used e-mail to set everything up, then an e-mail to thank them will be acceptable. If it is a very formal company, mail a typed letter. This will demonstrate that you are a professional. My personal favourite (and a very effective approach) is a handwritten thank-you note. It shows that you've taken the time and effort to address the employer specifically, and it's very personal. It's a warm kind of letter to receive, and helps to solidify a positive relationship with the hiring manager and the other people involved.

Choosing the right message is crucial to writing a successful thank-you letter. Start off by thanking the person for their time and for giving you the opportunity to meet with them. Highlight some of the topics that you discussed in the interview and provide them with any additional information they may have asked for. Your last paragraph is crucial: reiterate your interest in the company and the position and the reasons that you're a good fit. Hiring managers are busy people. Be clear, concise and direct, and demonstrate clearly why you are a good answer to their needs.

If you had an informational interview, your thank-you might look like this: "I just wanted to thank you for talking with me yesterday. It was very helpful with my job-search efforts. I much appreciated your taking the time out of your busy schedule to do this. Best wishes to you."

Or your letter might look like this: "I wanted to write and thank you for considering me for the position of XXX that I interviewed for yesterday. If you have any other questions that will help clarify my suitability for this exciting job opportunity, I would be happy for the chance to talk to you again. I look forward to hearing from you about further interviews or the outcome of the interviewing process. Best wishes."

Timing is everything. Don't wait until you "get a chance to do it." Your letter can go out as early as a few hours after the interview. Every day that you hold off puts you further from the process — think of the old expression, "Strike while the iron is hot." Even if you don't end up getting the job, you will have left a good impression with the people involved in the process. They may contact you with another opportunity, consider you for a position at a later date or refer you to one of their friends or peers.

CHAPTER FIVE

THE JOURNEY BEGINS

There are two basic job-search methods: the classic method and the "right job" method. While I strongly recommend the latter, it *is* more time-consuming and difficult. But in the end, the right job search has a higher probability of finding you a job that will be your best fit. Which method is best for you?

THE CLASSIC JOB SEARCH

The classic job search promises that you can find a job in three easy steps:

- Prepare your résumé.
- Post your résumé on the Internet and read the online classifieds or newspaper ads.
- Prepare your cover letter and résumé to reflect the needs of the job postings and apply.

Ninety percent of all job hunters conduct a classic job search, yet only 10 to 25 percent of all available jobs are advertised in newspapers or on job sites such as Working.com, Workopolis.com or Monster.ca. You need to explore further. Other possible resources include local websites that could be focused on jobs in your target area. Try a Google search combining your city of interest with the keyword "jobs" — for example, "Peterborough + jobs" — or a variation of this. Use an Internet search engine to gather information on the company that is publicly available. If you have certain companies in mind, go directly to their websites; some companies, both big and small, post job ads directly on their website and nowhere else.

Finally, read newspapers — specifically, the classified section, although the news and editorial sections may also give you some job leads or names of contact people to pursue. If you are looking for a job in a different city, get the local paper. Most newspapers have websites, and many post their classified ads online.

HOW TO READ THE WANT ADS EFFECTIVELY

- Pick a certain time every week (or a couple of times a week) to read, compile and reply to the ads. It is easier to reply to ten ads when you are on a roll than to reply to one or two at a time on a piecemeal basis.
- Scan job boards and the classifieds.
- Read for insight. You may not see jobs in your field, but you may see ads from companies you are interested in. Make a note and keep track of the information.
- Keep a record of the job ads you respond to.
- Keep electronic copies of the cover letters you create for the ads.

The Opportunity Tracking Tool below will help you track the jobs you have applied for.

OPPORTUNITY TRACKING TOOL
Date of Ad:
Date Responded:
Job Title:
Company:
Website:
Name:
Date of Interview:
Follow-Up:
Action Items:

If you are in a growing or booming field, you may come across more jobs than you can possibly apply for. Carefully choose which ones you apply for, but if you have time, apply for as many as you can. Don't waste a great deal of time applying for jobs you are clearly over- or underqualified for. For instance, to cite a couple of extreme examples, a paramedic would have no business applying for a surgeon's position, while it would be equally inappropriate for a high-tech executive to apply for a job in a stock room. However, you may need to apply for a job you are overqualified for, especially when you want to break into a new industry or career field. A step down may be necessary to get you that all-important first job in a new field. Apply for jobs that:

- meet your qualifications and experiences, passions, talents and desired lifestyle
- you would accept if offered
- genuinely interest you

Applying for a job, even using the classic job-search strategy, takes time, especially if you need to research the company. Choose wisely and do a great job on a few applications, rather than a crummy job on many.

When should you reply to the ad? The ideal time frame is two to three days after the ad appears. But take note: it has been determined that looking at old job ads from three to four months before and applying for them sometimes works. The person who was hired may not be working out, or they may be so busy that they are in the position to hire others, and your résumé may arrive as a godsend. Plus, you won't be competing against a whole host of other, solicited résumés.

E-MAILING RÉSUMÉS AND COVER LETTERS: FIVE THINGS TO THINK ABOUT

- *Subject Line.* Use the subject line wisely. Think of it as your headline; be sure to mention the hiring manager's name as well as the purpose of your e-mail.
- *File Names.* Include your own name in the name of any file you attach to your message. A file with a name like AlanKearns_Resume.doc makes it easier for employers to recognize and find.
- *Virus Check.* Keep your virus-scanning software up to date, and remember to *use it* — your computer system may be infected with a virus without you even knowing it. It's imperative that your messages and attachments be free of viruses — otherwise, the server at the recipient's office will block your e-mail and it will never arrive at its destination.
- *E-mail Address.* You've taken great pains to make sure your résumé presents you in the best possible light. But your e-mail address is the first thing a potential employer will see, so it should also make a positive first impression. If your e-mail handle is "cute" or "cool" — or less than business-friendly — it's time for a change. If possible, pick a new one that includes your real name or some recognizable variation.
- *Content.* Use the body of the e-mail as your cover letter. Make it short and to the point, but be sure to include any information the company is asking for. Always spell check your message, and don't be too casual.

THE "RIGHT JOB" SEARCH

The remainder of this chapter deals with my preferred job-search method. While it is straightforward, it is not easy. It will take time and effort, but by following this strategy you will be able to access the hidden job market. The different approaches set out in the rest of this chapter have been developed by conducting extensive research into the successful efforts of North American job hunters, using the best parts of each.

The "right job" search strategy has a higher success rate and it will help you uncover more opportunities and increase your chances of getting hired. Between 80 and 90 percent of available jobs do not appear on websites, newsgroups, or in classified ads. The majority of jobs exist in the hidden job market. Therefore, the classic job-search method misses many opportunities. This is why I recommend that you spend the majority of your time following the right job search methodology.

TARGETING

Before you get started, you need to know where the job opportunities are. Using the right job description you created earlier, make a list of the companies where you might find a niche. Use the Internet, magazines and your business contacts to help identify potential targets. Keep in mind the other aspects of your right job that you have identified, including location, salary and environment. Here's the type of information you should gather:

- history and potential growth for employer and industry
- restructuring, downsizing, re-engineering
- products and services
- location
- revenues and trends with respect to industry trends
- major competitors
- management structure
- size of the company
- purpose, funding levels and activities (if the employer is a non-profit organization)
- typical career path of an employee in this company
- training and development offered to staff
- technology used by company
- recent changes in management, and the effects of the changes

- annual reports, newsletters and articles written on the company
- employer's position in the field (is it new and innovative, or old and seeking to revitalize and re-establish market share?)
- name and contact information of the person who does the hiring

The Company Research Tool below compiles the contact information needed for your search. This information will help you identify specific challenges, problems or issues that may motivate the hiring manager to want to meet with you.

COMPANY RESEARCH TOOL
Company name:
Profit or non-profit/not-for-profit?
If non-profit, how is it funded?
Location of other plants/offices:
Company's financial status:
Is part or all of the company unionized? If yes, by whom?
What are the company's products?
What are the company's services?
What parts of the company's activities are carried out where I am applying?
Age of organization:
Current situation in the field:
Size of company:
Friends/contacts in the company:
Name and correct designation of hiring manager:
What is the company's pre-employment testing policy?
Potential problems the company is having:
How I can help to fix them:
Other information:

From those companies you have researched, pick the ten where you might be able to create your right job. Using the Right Job Target Chart below, list the detailed contact information.

RIGHT JOB TARGET CHART					
Rank	Position	Company Contact	Internal Manager	Person Hiring	Contact Information
1					e-mail: phone:
2					e-mail: phone:
3					e-mail: phone:
4					e-mail: phone:
5					e-mail: phone:
6					e-mail: phone:
7					e-mail: phone:
8					e-mail: phone:
9					e-mail: phone:
10					e-mail: phone:

APPROACH LETTERS AND CALLS

Approach Letters

After identifying the ten companies you want to work for, make contact with each via an approach letter. Use the knowledge you have gathered about each company to form the content of your letter. Use high-quality paper and don't send an e-mail; the letter is a tangible entity that sits on someone's desk and must compel him or her to read. Remember that this letter is only the first contact; you must follow up with a phone call.

Since you will need practice in this process, start with the company you favour the least. Save the companies you are most interested in until you have gained a bit of experience. Read the examples that follow to get an idea of what works and what doesn't, but write the letter in your own words. Experts say that this process takes three rounds of rewriting. Capture something in the first paragraph that resonates with the addressee. Be aware of the job and training of the reader and write your letter in a way that will speak to them. Ideally, you want to find a problem within the company that you can solve and thus become invaluable. If you have some insight in this area, don't be afraid to focus on this "challenge issue."

Example 1

Dear Dr. Jones:

Your company's XYZ technology is impressive. The fuel cell powering the AUV, as outlined in the February 28 edition of the *National Post*, is at the forefront of alternative energy applications.

Over the last twenty years I've built a very successful partnership practice as an optometrist and am now looking for a new challenge based on my passion for the frontiers of alternative energy technology — fuel cells for vehicles, hydrogen fuel cells and solar electrolysis for hydrogen production.

I would like to learn more, particularly about commercialization of your technology and the opportunities for entry into new markets. I'm excited about the future of fuel cells for businessmen like myself, and your observations would be helpful.

I would like to meet you in person and ask some questions. At this point, my visit is for information, not for a job.

I will call in a few days to arrange a meeting. I appreciate the value of your time, so be assured that I will take no more than thirty minutes.

Sincerely,

Example 2

Dear Mr. Michaels:

John Hancock (Company XYZ employee) indicated you might be interested in discussing some of the product development challenges Company XYZ will be facing in the near future.

I have twenty-two years' experience as an engineering analyst, system developer and software developer. My machine vision experience has been developed as a result of six years as senior analyst at Company ABC, working primarily on their space vision system. This is a video-based measurement system used in the assembly of the International Space Station.

What I have learned is that there are often specific problems that can delay projects and add costs. For example, when adding new functionality to the algorithmic core of a machine vision system, particular attention must be paid to:

1. Effective algorithm design to achieve the required level of performance with a high level of confidence, within constraints such as execution time. The danger is an inadequate design whose deficiencies are revealed only after the product is fielded. The key factors to success are:
   • clear statement of the requirements (the goal: good understanding of the problem domain, which in the case of machine vision consists of the scene being viewed, the optical system and the electronic imaging system); and
   • algorithm design based on sound fundamental principles.

2. Efficient testing to demonstrate that the required level of performance has been met. The pitfall here is to set up a complex test, gather gigabytes of data, and then realize that the test objective cannot be met. The keys to success are:
   • identifying the performance indicators (often just one or two numbers) up front; and
   • planning the data analysis before the data is gathered.

As an example of effective algorithm design, I developed a simple automatic target-acquisition algorithm to find the space vision system target dots in video of the space station. This algorithm used an extremely fast method to identify candidate dots, then relied on the space vision system's existing criteria for deciding which candidates were real dots. This satisfied the customer's requirements with a minimum of development effort and very little computation. Perhaps you are facing other challenges. I know I'd enjoy talking about them with you. I'll call in a few days to arrange a day and time to meet.

Yours sincerely,

Approach Calls

Once you've sent the letter, follow up with a phone call. The keys to this call are the three Ps: professional, personal and persistent.

You will face obstacles in getting the appointment. When you run into difficulty, don't be discouraged, be persistent! Once you reach the secretary or assistant, the conversation will go something like this: "Hello, my name is _____ and I would like to speak with _____."

The assistant may give you one of three answers: "He/she is not in"; "He/she is busy"; or "One moment please."

If he/she is not in, say, "Fine, I would like to leave my number." If busy, you say, "Fine, I'll call back. What's a good time?"

Always ask for the assistant's name, because you have then added to your contact list and added another relationship within the company.

If the assistant asks, "What is this concerning?" your response should be truthful and concise. "Mr./Ms. _____ is expecting my call." And this is true; just remember the last paragraph of your letter. The assistant may say, "Let me put you through to the personnel department." If this happens, respond, "That won't be necessary, since I am not calling to apply for a job." This is also true: you are *not* applying for a job — not yet, anyway. Currently, you are investigating the company.

THE INFORMATIONAL INTERVIEW

Remember above all else that the informational interview is not a job interview. When you are seeking this type of interview, ask for fifteen to twenty minutes of the person's time. Recognize that many job seekers are also trying to schedule informational interviews, so you may be turned down. If, on the other hand, you are granted the meeting, keep to the time frame. Define a focus and a goal for the meeting. The ultimate goal is to identify the company's problems, so that you can be a problem-solver, an invaluable asset.

You don't want to come across as someone begging for a job. During the interview, try to limit the amount that you talk; if the employer asks you a question, limit your response to between twenty seconds and two minutes, no more! When your twenty minutes are up, thank the employer and leave, unless the employer insists that you stay. Use a line like "I said I would only require twenty minutes of your time, and I recognize that you are very busy." This shows your respect for the employer.

Bring copies of your résumé to the interview. If the opportunity arises, you can provide the potential employer with vital information about your experience. Since you are going to an interview without a specific job in mind, create the résumé to reflect the skills you think may address the needs and wants of the company. Have a "sound bite" or specific sentence or two to describe you. Make it concise, and include important information that may pique the employer's interest in you and your ability to fit into their company.

What should you wear? Dress on the conservative side. Business suits are safe, and recommended. As part of your research, ask about the company dress code. At the very least, make sure your clothes are clean and presentable.

As you begin to develop a rapport with your potential employer, move from the general questions about the industry to personal matters and company affairs. Move back and forth, being sensitive to individual reactions. This process will lead you to your goal.

The following are examples of questions to ask during your interview. You will not have time to ask all of these questions; however, several will be crucial to get the information you need. Let's begin with a list of personal questions. Bear in mind that these are generalized examples that will give you some ideas about the scope of your questioning and establish the proper tone and approach. Your own questions will be more focused and refined, and therefore more appropriate for the individual situation.

Personal Questions

- In the last year, which of your contributions to your firm are you most proud of? In the last five years?

- What person (or persons) you recruited have impressed you the most?
- What attributes are necessary for success for a person in your position?
- How have you changed the nature of your job?
- What are your short-range objectives? Your long-range objectives?
- What professionals in your field do you admire most and why?
- If you could do whatever you wish professionally, what would that be? What would it mean for your organization? What prevents you from doing it?
- What feature of this position would you change or eliminate?
- What development has occurred in your field that you did not envision in your career plans? What has this development meant for your future and the future of others in this field?
- What does increased government activity mean to your profession?
- If you had to do it all over, would you join the same field and the same organization? Why or why not?
- What is the opinion of professionals you respect about the growth potential in your field in the next five years?

Industry Questions

- What factors are responsible for the positive or innovative trends in the industry? Are they social, political or individual trends?
- What factors are responsible for the growth of the industry?
- What specific research has the industry found useful in terms of product growth?
- How has the development of the industry come about, and what new strategy is being used to continue or diversify that development?
- What is the overall earning potential of your industry?
- What about government regulation in the industry — is it a plus or a minus?

- Are you affected by environmental restraints? Do any interest groups affect the work you do?
- Is your growth fast or slow? Is it typical of the field?
- How about supplies or suppliers and personnel? What material-supply problems are there? Are you able to attract and keep good people?
- What specific trends affect you (markets drying up, hostility towards the industry, cost factors, etc.)?
- Do you have too much competition? Too little? Why is the competition better or worse?

Company Questions

- What is the overall philosophy of management in your organization? How is it specifically implemented? How can you personally measure that philosophy?
- How accurately are new development and markets perceived, and what is the management style? Open, vertical, horizontal?
- What are the long- and short-range goals of the company?
- How are profits maximized? Through improved cost-cutting, marketing, strategy, superior product, or service?
- What has been the major achievement of the company in the marketplace?
- What makes your company better than others in the same field?
- How does your firm respond to government regulation? What costs have been incurred as a result?
- Who is responsible for responding to government regulations?
- What other political factors are at work in the industry that affects your organization?
- How are you attracting employees to keep up with your growth? If growth is unusually fast: What markets will you lose if you cannot attract people? What particular skills and abilities do you look for to help you increase your share of profits and earnings?
- How is quality control maintained? By whom?
- What influence do inflationary trends have on you?

- What are you doing to capture and keep your share of the market?

Some Questions You May Be Asked

- Tell me about yourself.
- How did you come to get the information to contact me?
- Why have you contacted me?
- Why are you interested in our company/industry/career field?

Remember, keep your answers short — between twenty seconds and two minutes. After the interview, write down what you have learned and decide if you are still interested in working for the company. Detail the problems or opportunities you have identified and begin formulating a plan where you can begin working with them. Write a thank-you card and mail it. Consolidate the information you have gathered using the Informational Interview Review below.

INFORMATIONAL INTERVIEW REVIEW
Interview with company:
What I learned about the interviewee:
What I learned about the company:
Stated needs to company:
Ways that I can fill those needs:
Potential problems I can solve:
Action items and follow-up:
Other information gathered:
Thank-you card sent:

JOB SHADOWING

Job shadowing is a slightly different approach to the informational interview, and one that may not be appropriate to your life stage or job type. If you have good contacts within the company you are seeking a job in, this may be ideal. As you have done for the informational interview, make contact with the person who has the power to hire you, and request an opportunity to shadow them over the course of a half or full day of work. The advantages are obvious: you have an increased opportunity to make contact and establish relationships, and to impress them with your knowledge and/or skills. In this case, the ante is much higher as you are in their space, so be self-aware, self-confident and sensitive to the people you are interacting with.

The job-shadowing opportunity can be a good follow-up to a successful informational interview. After the interview, you should have information on the company as well as knowledge of the problems and opportunities it faces. Job shadowing gives the employer a chance to see you interact in, and add to, the workplace. If you arrange a job-shadowing session, send thank-you notes both to the person you shadowed and their boss (if they are different people).

Do you remember taking field trips in school? They offered a break from routine, the chance to meet new people and learn new things, and sometimes, extra treats were thrown in. One of my clients discussed his idea of a "career field trip," reframing the informational interview and job-shadowing experience as the career field trip. He knew it would bring the same benefits, but also adventure and fun.

Experiencing a new work environment can change our perspective on a particular company and/or industry. A career field trip is like a backstage pass — you can get a good sense of the organization and/or role before you jump in. The more field trips you go on, the more chances you will have to build relationships and meet new people.

Have you taken any career field trips? What have you learned from them? What kind of opportunities have arisen as a result? What new relationships have developed? Look around to see if there are any companies where you can take a career field trip. You might be surprised at how much of an adventure research can be!

SEBASTIAN MANAGÒ: WORKING TO LIVE, NOT LIVING TO WORK

"In a big city and a big company, many things are taken care of. Your place is defined. There are lots of opportunities for little cogs in big wheels, but this can be distracting. You never think about what you want to do."

Sebastian grew up in Germany in a publishing family. As a young adult he chose to move to Canada for his education and earned a bachelor's degree in comparative literature before completing an MBA in France. Next there was a move to Spain, where he joined the international publishing firm Bertelsmann. From there, he was transferred to the firm's book club division, headquartered in New York.

Working in publishing suited Sebastian well — "I was like the butcher's son who liked meat" — and he was successful from the get-go. He began with the Military Book Club, where he doubled sales. He moved to product development and market research, which helped him understand the how and why of the way things worked. He was later made responsible for all of the niche book clubs and eventually was accountable for the flagship Literary Guild.

Sebastian considered himself a marketing person. He could have sold anything, but he found books far more interesting than anything else. After a brief stint in Toronto, he moved back to New York, where he enjoyed living, and to Random House, reporting to the chairman. During the dot-com craze of the late '90s, he was recruited to a senior position at Circle.com, a direct-to-consumer advertising agency. Sebastian was involved in many different projects, one of the most prestigious of which was the launch of the Mini automobile brand in North America.

In 2001, Sebastian decided he wanted to focus more on his personal life than his career. He jumped at the opportunity to work remotely for the agency from his summer home, on 500 acres in Prince Edward Island. The laid-back atmosphere — and absence of traffic jams — appealed greatly. But in September of that year, he was offered a position he couldn't refuse — heading the agency in Paris, where he would work with such clients as Peugeot. However, in 2002 the agency was shut down, so Sebastian returned to PEI.

This transition took its toll on his self-confidence. Over the next two years, questions began to trouble him: *What are you good for? What can you achieve? What are your talents?* "I was much more naive about the reality of what can be done. I began to doubt all the things I'd believed, developed a sense of dark disappointment. In a big city and a big company, many things are taken care of. Your place is defined. There are lots of opportunities for little cogs in big wheels, but this can be distracting. You never think about what you want to do. Career momentum takes over."

Sebastian learned that when you move to a smaller environment, you are on your own; therefore, you have to create your own ladder to climb your own wall. "You have to create your own opportunities." He also learned that you must be very secure in yourself, and that the faster you figure out what you want to do, the more rapidly you will get on your way.

The adjustment has changed Sebastian in many ways, but he has found his path. He is involved in a consulting role with the University of PEI as well as a number of thriving direct-to-consumer projects, including a smoked salmon company.

It is not about the money. Money is fine, but the drive to earn a lot of it doesn't translate directly into job satisfaction. As Sebastian has learned, you need to concentrate on what you really know and where you really want to live.

NETWORKING

Eric Morse, the J.R. Shaw Professor of Entrepreneurship at the University of Western Ontario's Richard Ivey School of Business, is one of Canada's leading thinkers in the area of the value of networks. He hasn't just spent a lot of time researching networking; it is also something that he has experienced personally, both in his work with entrepreneurs and his own career. "One of the things we have discovered is that opportunities come about by what you know and who you know. When those two things come about, you will uncover things that others may not see. It is amazing when you are open, and in my four years at the Ivey School of Business I have seen it time and time again."

Opportunity arises out of the combination of what you know and who you know. According to some statistics, more than 70 percent of job opportunities come from knowing people in the market.

What you know. What do you have to offer the global market? The job market today is looking for very specific knowledge. It could come in many different ways — through executive development, formal certification, a master's degree, an MBA or even a Ph.D. The more you develop your expertise in your area, the more value you will have to offer your network, and the more your network will want to connect with you.

Who you know. There are different types of networks. There are people you meet at a party and exchange business cards with. These contacts may lead to new opportunities. There are also embedded relationships: these are ongoing ones, particularly over the longer term, with people in whom you have a high level of trust. These embedded relationships are especially important and will likely offer you the most opportunities more quickly and more efficiently. Embedded relationships are usually built on time and infrastructure. The infrastructure could be alumni networks, community associations, churches or people you have worked with over a long period of time.

It takes time to develop and shape your network. We get so busy that we don't take time to think about it. Ask yourself a couple of questions: With your experience and contacts, who do you need to know? What skills do you need to have? Once you take stock of the things you need to be successful, put yourself in situations where you will be around people who can make that happen. Who are the leading thinkers in the area you want to be in? These people can serve as a gateway to the field you want to move into. Pick up the phone and give them a call. You will be amazed how many people will respond and want to meet with you.

COMMON EXCUSES FOR NOT NETWORKING

- I don't think it's fair … you should hire the best candidate.
- I don't know how to network.
- I don't have a very established network.
- I don't have the time.
- Professionals in my network won't have the time.
- I am not sure what I would have to offer people in my network.
- I don't think it really works.
- Later in my career is a better time to network.
- It's more time-effective to go online.
- I don't like it.

Building networks is all about preserving your options, both for yourself and your business as you move forward. Don't underestimate the value of what you have. Your experience, education and unique perspective are literally one in six billion. Think of the unique value of Bill Gates. How many people could have accomplished what he has? Think about your unique value proposition — what is the thing that you have to offer the market that nobody else has? The reason Bill Gates is so valuable (other than the $40 billion he has in the bank) is that there is only one of him. There is far more demand for him than there is supply.

Opportunities that are created through a network are most often shaped around an individual rather than a fixed job description. Not that a job description is a bad thing, but in my many years in this field, I have observed that it is far easier — and much more effective — to shape a job description around an individual than to find a person who fits the description. This principle also increases the sense of fit for the obvious reason that companies are hiring *you* ... not a job description. When you are out networking or at a conference, both you and the employer are more likely to uncover each party's needs and start a discussion that could lead to a project — or even the presidency of a new venture.

Networking is invaluable. Building relationships with individuals and groups of people who can assist you in planning your career is vital to your success. Networking is not only for extroverted job-seekers. It is certainly more difficult for shy people, but it is still critical. You can work on creating your network through personal meetings, the telephone or via the Internet. Having a network is important in accessing the hidden job market.

Networking occurs on three levels. Level I consists of people you talk to frequently, such as close friends or family. These are people you'll feel comfortable about approaching to ask for names of people *they* know who may be able to help you. At Level II are the people you describe as colleagues or acquaintances. You might know them from the health club or from your child's hockey team. Included on this list should be your doctor, lawyer and other professionals whose services you use. Finally, there's Level III: people you don't know but who you believe might be able to help you. The best way to get in touch with these people is to use a Level I or II contact. If you can obtain their contact information, you may be able to set up an informational interview.

Who is in your network? Use the Network Target List at the end of this section to list the people who are currently in your network and those you plan to add to it. Ask the following three questions about each contact on the list you create:

- Do they have hiring authority?
- Can they share any job leads?
- Can they refer you to others?

The ultimate goal of this process is to create links to people with hiring authority. Do not dismiss people who do not have hiring authority, as they may know someone who does the hiring, or they may have valuable information about the industry or company you are focusing on.

As you contact different people in your network, keep a record of the status of the relationship, make a note of when you phone, leave a voice mail or send e-mail. Send your contacts thank-you cards, even if the contact hasn't been fruitful. You never know who they may give your name to.

THREE NETWORKING MYTHS

- **Only those people who can offer you the job are worth networking with.**
- **You have to know the "right people" to network effectively.** How do you identify these people? The "wrong person" might be married to the "right one."
- **Strangers resent it when you ask for help in your job search.** Sometimes people don't have the time, and they'll rudely let you know. But the majority will be flattered to help as long as you are polite and appreciative.

Your Networking Sales Pitch

Your pitch should pique the listener's attention. It should provide some useful information to help them decide whether they would like to talk to you, and it should inform them of how they can help you. Your pitch should last no longer than twenty-five seconds. Record yourself and listen to the way you speak and your tone.

The pitch includes:

- your name
- your profession or occupation
- your current job status (employed, unemployed, looking for new challenges)

- what sort of opportunities you are seeking
- what distinguishes you from others

While it can be challenging to fit all of this information into a clip lasting twenty-five seconds, it is possible with practice and editing. For the purposes of the telephone networking pitch, you need to reduce the clip to two parts, one being your name and how you got their name. After they respond and state that they have time to talk, you can present the remainder of the pitch.

A sample networking sales pitch sounds something like this: "Hello, my name is _____. _____ gave me your name and suggested that I contact you. For the past __ years, I have been working as a _____ and have specialized in _____. Right now I am _____ and I am looking for _____. What I have to offer is _____."

Remember to work with the framework above and adapt it to reflect you and your style.

Examples of Telephone Pitches

"Hello, my name is Rochelle Martin, and I got your name from Julia Churchill. Do you have a minute or two to talk with me? [*After you get permission to move ahead.*] I've been an epidemiologist for more than five years, working mainly with pharmaceutical safety. My former firm, AB&C, went through a restructuring a few months ago and has disbanded my department. Now I am looking to join a medium-sized agency that handles health promotion. I have lots of contacts in the field, and I know I could help a company build its business."

"Hello, my name is John Davidson, and I got your name from Tanya Guenther. Do you have a minute or two to talk with me? [*After you get permission to move ahead.*] I graduated from university last April with a degree in computer science and have spent the past four months as a temporary chip designer with XYZ Networks. I am looking for an entry-level engineering position in a corporation that has international offices, specifically in Latin America. I am fluent in Spanish and Portuguese, and because I lived in Brazil for several years, I have a good sense of how to do business in South America."

MY NETWORK TARGET LIST
Name:
Title:
Company:
Business Address/Phone:
Home Address/Phone:
E-mail Address:
Fax Number:
Nature of Connection:
Level of Contact (I, II or III):
Status of Relationship:
Their Priority in My Job Search:
Other Companies to Which They Have Connections:
Additional Names They Have Given Me:
Additional Comments:

RECRUITERS

Recruiters, or headhunters, can add significant value to both the candidate and the employer. They often specialize in specific areas of the job market, which gives them a deep understanding of the people, technology and trends in these areas. They have established relationships with many people with hiring authority, from senior technical personnel all the way up to CEOs, who are often focused on their own day-to-day responsibilities and therefore may not be aware of many of the candidates who are available. Many of the positions the recruiter represents are never advertised, therefore they have the "inside scoop" on many companies, something that is even more relevant for positions at the senior management level.

Recruiters also offer job seekers an additional channel, because they have insights and information about jobs that most people can't access completely on their own, especially those who are balancing their search with the needs of everyday life. You would have nothing to lose, and hopefully much to gain, by getting yourself onto the radar screen of a third-party search firm.

The greatest benefit that recruiters offer is that they are often instrumental in bringing employers and top talent together. They are skilled at negotiating the various details of the offer stage, an area that is usually the most complex part of the hiring process, and one that many companies — and individuals — have difficulty managing successfully.

When you approach a recruiter, it is extremely important that you be vigilant; some are in it solely for the money and will circulate your résumé without your permission. Before signing on, ask for references — and then contact them — to determine the integrity and quality of the recruiter.

If you are thinking of working with a recruiter, ask them the following questions:

- How long have you been a recruiter?
- How does the process work?
- What is your placement success rate?
- What industry specialties and areas of expertise do you and your company focus on?
- Are you currently working on any job orders that my skills could match?
- Do you send résumés to clients first, or do you get approval from the candidate first?
- When/how often should I be in contact with you?

There are also questions that recruiters should ask you to ensure that they understand you and your situation. They should ask you about relocation factors, your family, salary requirements and the positions you would be interested in interviewing for. It is very important that you feel a chemistry with the recruiter. Their salaries are paid by the employers, so they may not have your best interests at heart.

Here are some myths about recruiters:

They work for you. They will help you, but they are paid by employers to help them grow their companies. The company is the client, not you!

They will help you shift sectors A big part of the reason that employers use recruiters is to shorten the timeline to hire and to access a specific network of skilled candidates, those who have what I call "start tomorrow skills." Recruiters are looking for what their clients want, which is people who already have a background in a sector. Therefore, they won't be broadening their search to include people with experience in other disciplines.

They will help manage your career. They can give great advice, but they are rewarded for their ability to help companies to hire. In other words, they are motivated to fill vacancies, not to develop talent.

They will negotiate on your behalf. They *can* do this, but ultimately they must deliver what their client wants. It's in their interest to adhere as closely as possible to the parameters of the employer's offer.

There are two key types of relationships that recruiting firms have with their employer clients: *contingency* and *retained*. A contingency relationship is one in which a company uses a number of recruiters, in addition to their own website and networks. The recruiter doesn't have an exclusive relationship with the employer, and the employer will hire whoever they wish from wherever they can find the best candidate. In a sense, this is similar to selling a home through the Multiple Listing Service, where any real estate agent can sell a property. The other type is an exclusive relationship between the employer and a single recruiting agency. Under this arrangement, the recruiter is authorized to act on the company's behalf as the first decision-maker, so it is important that you understand and treat this relationship with the appropriate care. There is no other way to access an opportunity at the company other than through this recruitment agency.

Remember that the recruiter is ultimately paid by the employer; as a result, he or she is working in the best interests of the company. This isn't a bad thing, but it is important to understand that the employer will be charged a percentage of your first year's salary (anywhere from 15 to 30 percent, depending on the relationship the recruiter has developed). Professional recruiters can open doors for you and give you access to a world of wonderful opportunities you might not otherwise be aware of. The key is to keep your options open and develop relationships with several of them — don't rely on just one.

FIVE SECRETS TO GETTING A RECRUITER ON YOUR SIDE

- *Have a great reputation.* Recruiters are always asking who is good and who is looking. The best way to get recruiters to call you is to be great at what you do.
- *Treat them with respect.* If you are contacted by a recruiter, even if you are not looking, take some time to chat and be pleasant. You may not be the right fit this time, but this contact could be the foundation for a long-term relationship.
- *Pay attention to packaging and presentation.* Make it easy for them to sell you: have a great résumé and present yourself well.
- *Relationship, relationship, relationship.* Relationships are about trust and openness. If you are open and trustworthy, you will get a good reputation in the "recruiter subculture" and you will be called on again and again.
- *Talk, don't stalk.* Recruiters are busy people. Sometimes they need a friendly reminder that you are in the market, but don't be a pest.

HUMAN RESOURCES DEPARTMENTS

Many organizations have human resources departments, and the people who work here can be allies during your job search. Quite often, before they will answer even a simple query, they will ask you to complete a job application form. When completing such a form, be sure to do the following:

- Use a black pen.
- Print neatly.
- Answer every question (even those that aren't applicable).
- Write "open" for salary expectations.
- If asked why you left your last job, you may say that the job ended; it was seasonal; it was temporary; you are looking for a career change; or you wanted more responsibility than your last job offered.

CHAPTER SIX

THE JOB INTERVIEW AND LANDING THE RIGHT JOB

Lately, you have spent countless hours crafting résumés and cover letters, networking, assessing yourself and visualizing about finding joy in a job. Because of your hard work and risk-taking, you will be asked to attend a job interview.

Employers view the job interview as an opportunity to get to know you, the applicant, to gauge whether you have the skills and abilities they need and to assess how well you might fit in with the company's culture. But it's also a valuable experience for you: on the one hand, it's your opportunity to show that you are the best person to fulfill the company's needs; on the other, it's a chance to learn more about the company and decide whether it's the kind of place you want to work. Most people are uncomfortable in an interview situation — even the interviewers! — so it's not surprising that this is one of the areas in which I'm called upon to help coach clients the most. To perform effectively in an interview, remember the four Cs: confidence, chemistry, content and capability.

Confidence. Confidence is not to be confused with cockiness. It's a belief in your ability to handle the task at hand. If you truly understand the demands of the job, and are certain of your ability to do it, you will radiate a sense of confidence, and this will assure the employer that you will be able to get the job done. Imagine that your son or daughter needs an operation, and you are meeting the surgeon at the hospital. Wouldn't you be looking for that sense of assurance that he or she is not only qualified, but is certain of his or her abilities? Most employers will decide within two minutes whether you have what it takes; you must reflect this sense of confidence.

Chemistry. Most hiring managers hire people they like. Try to find something you can connect on, whether through shared experiences or something outside the scope of the workplace. Do a quick visual scan of the interviewer's office for photos, art, or any other indicator of some of their interests.

Content. Make sure you understand what you have to offer the organization, both in terms of skills and knowledge of the specific role or industry. It is more impressive if you can clearly articulate your skills and how they relate to the role you are being interviewed for. The night before, review your résumé and, on a separate piece of paper, make a bullet-point list of elements from your employment history that are relevant to the organization and role.

Capability. People are not hired if they are seen as bringing more risk than reward to the role. A hiring manager's greatest fear is that the person will fail in the role. Speak with your references and ask them to tell you what areas they feel you excel in. I call this the Ebert & Roeper "thumbs-up" effect. Most of us have gone to see movies based on recommendations from reviewers Roger Ebert and Richard Roeper on their syndicated TV show. If you enter the interview prepared with stories about your strengths, you will receive a thumbs-up evaluation.

You can always learn from an interview. You may not get the job you interview for, but you will learn about a company and meet some new people.

PREPARING FOR THE JOB INTERVIEW

You have researched the company that you will be interviewing with in your cover letter preparation stage. Now you need to expand that research to learn everything you can about the company and the person who will be interviewing you. If you haven't already done so, start by exploring the company's website to read its mission statement and press releases. Then search the web further or visit the library for more information about the organization. Use your contact network to glean anything else you can about the company.

Once you know a great deal about the company and your compatability, how do you communicate that knowledge? Being aware of the current situation of the company will allow you to frame your answers. If the firm is young and growing, you will want to highlight certain aspects of your character; on the other hand, if the firm is losing market share and scrambling to recoup, you will need to highlight other skills and qualities.

If you have presented yourself on your résumé as a smart, organized, professional, motivated and qualified candidate, be sure to present yourself the same way in an interview. The question to ask yourself before you meet a potential employer is, "Am I an effective communicator?" Effective speakers get their point across clearly and concisely in an interview. They grab attention and make strong points about themselves and their abilities in a short period of time.

To improve your answers in an interview setting, ask yourself the following questions:

What point am I trying to make? Listen to the questions, and answer them. Think about the outcome you want as a result of what you're about to say. If you start answering questions by going off on tangents, you will dilute your point and appear evasive and unfocused. With an objective in mind, you can focus on delivering a clear message that addresses the specifics of the question asked.

Am I stating my main ideas clearly? Make sure you back up your statements with examples — specific results, stories or statistics. Don't make a general comment without backing it up!

Do I know who I am speaking to? Remember why they invited you to the interview in the first place. What information are they looking for? Remember that people make decisions and judgements based on emotion. How do you want them to feel? How receptive is your listener to your ideas?

Do I start the interview with a powerful statement? Open with a statement that gets the interviewer's attention and summarizes what you're going to be talking about. This demonstrates that you are listening and that you understand what they've asked, and lets them know what points you're going to be addressing.

Am I an effective listener? Being an effective speaker means you also have to be an effective listener. If you aren't sure what the interviewer means, ask for clarification. Listen carefully to what the employer is saying so you can respond with relevant answers.

Do I finish strongly? Don't end your answer or statement with a disappointing, "Well, that just about does it." Integrate the points you've made in your opening statements. Your answers will stand out and won't leave doubt in the mind of the hiring manager.

Becoming a highly effective speaker takes work. With practice and proper attention, you will get better with every interview!

WILLIAM JANS: THE HYBRID CAREER

"If you have passion and tenacity, you are virtually unstoppable."

William Jans is one of Canada's foremost storytellers. Whether through his commercial photography or his storytelling events, he is a master of persuasion. Originally headed for a career in commercial art, he developed an interest in photography that led to a business. He has photographed such celebrities as Bill Cosby, Michael J. Fox and the members of The Clash.

In 1988 he travelled to Borneo for six weeks. Throughout his travels he did things he thought were interesting and sometimes absurd.

So, upon his return he rented a little community centre and invited friends and family to share the joys of his journeys. This is where his second career began.

William combines the travel slide show with videos, still photography and his own gift for storytelling, injecting his political and cultural perspectives. More than 20,000 people have seen his shows in Toronto, Vancouver, Edmonton, Calgary and other places across the country. He sold out an 847-seat theatre in Vancouver nine times — people waited in line for two to three hours for tickets.

William firmly believes that "if you have passion and tenacity, you are virtually unstoppable." This special combination of attributes served him well in his career as a commercial photographer. So when he was told that there were already two people in Vancouver doing concert photography and that there was no more room, William created a third spot for himself. He heard what others said, but did what he thought was right. "I have the good fortune that people like what I do," he says. He has never asked for a job; he determines what he wants up front, and then does it.

Before becoming a storyteller, he refined his communication skills, having learned how to relate and communicate in a corporate environment. He has dealt with a wide variety of people and learned from observing different skills and techniques. He gathers material by picking places that intrigue him and his audience.

Storytelling, William says, is about you, but it isn't personal. "It is everything but the smell," he jokes. Can you pull them in and make them understand what you are all about?" Here are some of the guiding principles for his shows.

- *Prepare and plan*. One of William's shows can be a year in the making. He invests hundreds of hours working out every detail, from the script and the choice of video clips right down to what he wears. And he's never finished: the show is constantly evolving as he tweaks it here and there to make improvements.
- *Keep your language simple*. William's audiences tend to be looking for raw, simple images in his stories. We are in an "MTV generation where things happen really quickly. We live in a sound-bite world."

William's advice is to slow things down. Bring context into everything that you do. Make sure you don't lose your audience. There needs to be a clear beginning, middle and end to your story, otherwise it can all unravel in an instant. Put yourself in your audience's shoes.

- *Rehearse, rehearse, rehearse.* William cannot take the risk of not scripting his show; there are just too many things happening. And, as actors do, William spends many hours getting his lines down. Before an informational meeting or an interview, you need to get your career story down in a script format. This helps in a number of ways. I have conducted interviews in which the candidate got the timeline mixed up or forgot important details. If you can, get all the facts down into a compelling story. Get into a voice that you are comfortable with, and practise so you do not sound like you're reciting a script. Practice doesn't really make perfect, but it does make for the smoothest possible presentation.

- *Show and tell.* William's shows depend on a variety of elements, including a number of visual aids, to tell the story. In an interview, there are many items *you* can use to help tell your story: e-mail and letters from clients and peers; awards; sales reports; performance reviews; media coverage. You can create a portfolio that incorporates the most pertinent information. Use different types of technology if you wish, but make sure it works.

- *Be "The Real McCoy."* In William's words, "I get to say what I get to say!" That is, he gets to tell his story in a real and authentic way. For him, career success means not only pleasing an audience, but being happy with what he does. And William says he is ecstatic. "I still have pride in what I do."

INTERVIEW QUESTIONS

The majority of questions asked in the interview setting are aimed at getting the same information in slightly different ways: Who are you? How will you help the company? Will you fit in? Think about how you might answer the following questions, which are the kind you're likely to be asked in an interview.

- Why did you apply for this job?
- Why should we give you this job? How are you going to solve our problems?
- Who are you? What are your talents, passions, values and desired lifestyle?
- How are you different from the other candidates we are interviewing? How are you going to go the extra mile?
- Can we afford to hire you? (Note: Your objective will be to make them ask themselves the question, "How can we not?")

The next several pages consist of interview questions and possible answers. Consider each question and draft your own answers.

Enthusiasm Questions
"What is your greatest strength?"

This question is a strong determinant of how self-confident you are and how willing you are to sell yourself. Take this question seriously. Tailor your answer to the position you are pursuing. If your greatest strength is your mathematical skills and the job is in sales, you need to pick a more relevant strength.

> "If I had to pick just one strength, I would have to say it is my flexibility. I am not afraid of challenges, new projects, challenging customers, or being put on the spot to defend a decision. In my last position as an account executive, I worked independently from my home office and was solely responsible for customer relations, sales, product management, order control, problem resolution, and all administration. I was constantly handed new products, new deadlines and other challenges that I handled with ease. Because of my flexibility my territory was made the launch site for the company's last three new products in 1999."

"What is your greatest weakness?"

This is perhaps the most dreaded of all interview questions. This single question will determine whether you are a potential asset or a liability. Let's take a look at what you should never say and why.

Never choose a weakness that demonstrates your inappropriateness for the job! "Dealing with difficult people" is not the right answer for a customer service or team-oriented position. A weakness such as "spelling" should never be the greatest weakness for an administrative assistant. Note, however, that a weakness can be turned into a virtue. For example:

> "I believe that in any position requiring clerical skills, it is important to produce high-quality, error-free work. Because of this, I always proofread my work and use the spell check as a backup. For uncommon words, I keep a dictionary handy."

It is important to pick a weakness that (a) does not hinder your ability to do the job or fit in with the company, or (b) is a strength in disguise or represents an irrelevant weakness. Review the job criteria and ensure that you pick a weakness that will not interfere with your ability to do the job.

You are probably asking yourself, "What are some weaknesses that could be strengths in disguise?" These include being a people-pleaser, a workaholic, a self-critic or a new graduate or entry-level worker without a great deal of experience. Listen to these examples:

> "It's important to me that people get along in the workplace. In the past I always went the extra mile to help out so I wouldn't let anyone down. I'm not saying I no longer help others out; however, I've learned to be more assertive, to better recognize and prioritize projects and to know whether I can bail others out without jeopardizing my existing work."

> "On my first day in my last job, I came out of my office to discover everyone else had left and locked the door, leaving me locked in! That pretty much classifies my career. In taking things to extremes, I have found that it is easy to get burned out by not balancing my time. I have worked with a success coach and implemented a Franklin Day Planner

to better organize and schedule my time, making sure I achieve a balance so that I can be a more valuable player."

"I feel that my greatest weakness is that I am critical of my own work. I have always prided myself on producing excellent and error-free work. While this is beneficial to my job performance, it is possible to go to extremes. I have also found that I can easily waste time checking and rechecking. Now I am aware of what to look for, so I make a conscious effort to trust myself and not be so critical of my work. I know that there is a limit to proofreading."

"Some people would consider the fact that I have never worked in this field as a weakness. But being highly trainable and open-minded, I have no preconceived notions on how to perform my job. Working with your organization will give me the opportunity to learn the job the way you want it done, not the way I believe it ought to be done. I have no on-the-job experience, but I do bring extensive hands-on training and experience, which enhances my ability to learn quickly."

And here's an example of how to use a harmless weakness:

"I once read in a survey that most people ranked public speaking above snakes and death as their worst fear. I'd have to say that my greatest fear is speaking in front of a large group. I'm not afraid of speaking to small groups, but the idea of having to address a large group makes me nervous. I know that right now this isn't a critical issue to my career growth. I recently heard of a group called Toastmasters that helps its members gain public-speaking skills. I'm strongly considering joining this group, unless your company actually has a chapter that I could get involved in."

Let me also use an example that is frequently recommended but that never works:

"I'd have to say my greatest weakness is the vending machine. I just adore chocolate!"

Yes, you may get a chuckle, but the interviewer will still expect a real answer. This might be a good icebreaker, but be prepared to still present a more serious weakness.

"Why do you think you will be successful in this position?"

This success-indicator question requires that you sell yourself and your knowledge of the company. I hope you did your homework on this company before the interview. You should emphasize your value and demonstrate your knowledge, as they work together. For example, someone applying for a position as an independent contractor to run a résumé-writing service might say:

"I can be successful in this position because of my unique background in résumé writing and career development. I am a Certified Professional Résumé Writer with two degrees in technical and creative writing. This has allowed me to develop the ability to effectively interview clients and research their backgrounds while creating dynamic marketing résumés. I have balanced this professional writing ability with six years of experience as the director of a college job-placement program where I taught résumé writing, interviewing, and job search and professional development, as well as performing job placement of the graduates. Not only did I achieve the highest levels of job placement ever recorded by the college (98 percent within ninety days of graduation), but I also gained solid insight into what employers look for, what works and what doesn't."

"I believe I can be successful because I am entrepreneurial. I know that the success of this office will depend upon my ability to market your services, retain clients and implement revenue streams. If I am selected for the position, I have numerous ideas I would like to discuss that I feel will allow me to operate effectively but also increase office sales."

In a more traditional situation, you may be a recent graduate with no idea of how to sell yourself for the position. You might answer like this:

> "I believe that I will be successful in this position because I have 900 hours of hands-on training in medical transcription in a classroom environment at the XYZ Institute. (Open your portfolio to display a sample of work.) Here you can see several examples of medical records, dictation and reports I have produced in Microsoft Word. I have also excelled in my terminology courses, gaining a strong base in numerous disciplines. I have always been interested in cardiology and made it a personal goal to focus on that area. Because of that, I read the *Journal of Cardiology* to stay up-to-date with changes in the field, names of new pharmaceuticals and other innovations. I have an excellent basis in the discipline to transcribe the records of your cardiologists with ease. Also, I recently joined the American Association of Medical Transcriptionists and am pursuing certification."

Self-Direction Questions
"Where do you see yourself in five years?"

This question lets the employer know whether you are goal-oriented, have put thought into your career choice and future, and whether you plan on having a future in this field.

Once, as I was teaching an interviewing class, we were role-playing our way through a hypothetical interview. When I asked this question of a student who was interviewing for an office manager's position, she said, "Oh, I plan to be a flight attendant. If I can just get this job, I can save enough money to go to school!" This was the last thing she should have said. Telling an employer you are only using them is rarely a good idea.

Another bad answer to this question is, "Doing *your* job." Don't be fooled into believing this demonstrates ambition. Threatening your interviewer is rarely a successful approach. Another zinger to avoid: "I only want to work here to get enough experience to open my own company."

And finally, don't say, "I don't know"! Never, under any circumstances, indicate that you do not have a career plan.

Above all, don't panic when you field this question. Don't be afraid that the interviewer will think your goal is unreasonable. What is important is to show that you have a goal, that you have devoted some thought to your career path, whether you get there or not. It is a very good idea to rehearse your answer to this question. Here is an example:

> "Since I started in this industry three years ago, I have set numerous short- and long-term goals for myself. I have consistently met the smaller ones, such as becoming a certified career coach and writing a monthly newspaper column in the *XYZ Today*. I know that it would be beneficial to my future in this field if I were to complete my degree, gain licensing and become a nationally certified career counsellor. To this end, I have been accepted to the prestigious Masters in Career Counselling program at XYZ University, and have completed twenty-one credits to date. On this time line, I will surely have reached my goal to further myself in this industry."

"How did you prepare for this interview?"

This question tests your planning and preparation skills. If you took the right steps in your research and preparation, you can sell yourself and your interest in the company. Your answer gives you a chance to focus on how much you want to work for them. Don't sell yourself short with an answer like, "Well, I researched the company and dry-cleaned my suit." Try something like: "After I spoke with you, I wanted to learn a little more about your company so that I could determine exactly how I could meet your needs. Since I only had a few hours after we spoke, I made a few calls to colleagues familiar with your organization and visited the library to do some research. I was able to uncover some fascinating news and a few questions I hope to be able to ask you as well."

"Give an example of a situation in which you had to plan an event or project and explain how you handled it."

How nice that you have been asked to demonstrate an experience you have gone through. Show, in a step-by-step progression, how you planned, organized and co-ordinated a project.

> "When I was the Assistant Director of Career Planning at XYZ College, I was asked to establish an advisory committee of community leaders who could direct our educational and job-placement programs. I met with the director and reviewed my professional contacts to establish a list of potential advisors. After I had selected an appropriate date and time, I prepared and sent out invitations and followed up to answer questions and make a list of participants. I was successful in procuring a number of very influential participants, including the Manager of XYZ County Jobs and Benefits, the Director of XYZ County Small Business Development and the Business Recruiter for the Chamber of Commerce.
>
> "In the interim, I established a topic outline for the meeting, planned and ordered breakfast and co-ordinated any special needs with the college representatives. The meeting was extremely successful, with all advisors agreeing to participate quarterly. After the meeting, I wrote up a summary, followed up on ideas presented with the director, and sent thank-you letters to each participant. It was an exciting project that I am extremely proud of. In fact, the group is still meeting today, five years later."

Problem-Solving/Critical-Thinking Questions
"If you were hiring for this position, what traits would you look for in a candidate?"

Your answer will demonstrate your attention to detail, your emphasis on selling yourself and your ability to see the big picture. Don't just say, "I'd hire someone like me." Demonstrate your critical-thinking skills and rational thought processes with an answer that shows you understand what the employer is looking for.

"I believe there are certain traits that are universal to most positions. If I were hiring, I would want to select someone who would be a company team player — an individual who represents the company and can interact well with both customers and staff. In addition, I would want someone who was self-directed and able to learn and handle multiple tasks. I believe that if someone is professional and meets these criteria, then they are also adaptable and can meet organizational goals."

"Tell me about yourself."

Job seekers often go off in the wrong direction when answering this question, because they misread its purpose. This is a job interview, not a game show, so the interviewer is not looking for personal details. No employer is going to hire you because you have cute children or a wonderful spouse. In fact, that type of information could put you out of the running for the job. This question is your opportunity to make your two-minute sales pitch for the product that is you.

You might wish to start by answering the question with a question: "I would be glad to. Could you give me an idea of the type of information you would like to know?" By starting this way, you can direct your answer better and be more conversational.

"I was born and raised in XYZ County and have an excellent knowledge of the area as well as Central and ABC counties. During the last nine years with FGH Express, I have progressed through the positions of package loader, courier, dispatcher and team lead. In my most recent position, I have had the opportunity to complete numerous management-training programs, provide supervision and leadership to all positions within the station and participate in special projects in conjunction with senior and district managers. I enjoy being a lead and having the opportunity to empower and motivate my team. Last year I was commended for greatest team gains in productivity. I believe this experience and training has prepared me to take the next step and pursue a management position with Arco Trucking."

"If you could be an animal, what would you be and why?"

You didn't see this one coming, did you? This type of question is rarely asked anymore, but if it is, there are a few things you need to understand. First of all, this type of question is asked only to catch you off-guard. The interviewer knows you will have to say the first thing that comes to mind, which is unrehearsed and therefore true. Second, there is rarely a wrong answer. What matters is that you make sense of your answer, expressing it clearly. And finally, no matter what you say, it will tell the employer something about you.

The best way to answer is to avoid saying anything negative about yourself. In fact, you can use cats, lions and birds effectively if you "market and sell" your answer. For instance, "I'd be a bird because then I could fly overhead and get a look at the big picture."

My favourites are:

"I'd be a dolphin, because they are extremely intelligent, always seem happy, travel, stay in pods and have been known to come to the aid of people."

"I'd be a chameleon, because they quickly change to meet their environment."

"I'd be a cat, because they are extremely independent and require little care. However, they seem to intuitively know when you want them around."

When you are faced with a "kicker" question like this, take a moment before responding. You might have to start by saying, "What animal? Hmm, that's an interesting question. I'll have to think about that for a minute."

Communication Skills Questions
"How would you compare your verbal skills to your written skills?"

When most people hear this question, they conclude that they must compare the two and say which one is better. This is a trick to get you to show a weakness. You don't have to! Comparing doesn't mean hurting yourself. Consider an answer that displays your strengths:

> "In a position such as this, I think it is important to have both strong verbal and written skills. I like giving presentations, speaking to customers and expressing myself face-to-face. I also enjoy writing because it is a more lasting form of communication and gives you the opportunity to formulate and think through your answer."

Or, if you really feel that you are weak in an area, you might say:

> "Because of the importance of being able to communicate, I strive to make sure I have strengths in both areas. I also feel comfortable dealing with people face-to-face and over the phone. I don't mind written communications, either, because I can double-check my work and ensure its accuracy."

"How would you respond if you were asked to give a presentation to our customers?"

This question tests whether you are comfortable giving presentations, know how to give one, and enjoy dealing with customers. Some people have been known to panic at this question and at the thought of speaking to a group or interacting with customers. One woman actually said, "I don't like dealing with the public." Why, I ask you, was she interviewing for a customer service/sales position?

> "I would be honoured to think that, because of my knowledge of the company and its products, I would be asked to make a presentation

to the customers. Would you like to know the steps I might take in preparing for a presentation?"

Or:

"I wouldn't mind. I'd be nervous, but I would overcome that by making sure I was prepared by knowing my product, projecting possible questions or concerns, and practising to ensure I made a positive presentation."

"How do you get along with others?"

Your answer demonstrates your ability to interact with customers and co-workers. If you say, "I get along well with everyone," you will sound positive but unrealistic. You can't assume that the interviewer will read between the lines and understand that you mean, for instance, that you handle difficult people with ease. You will need to clarify your response.

If employees can't get along with customers or fit in with existing staff, they could be a problem. If you do have trouble getting along with others, don't lie about it in the interview. Arrange to get professional help, as it will benefit you and impress a potential employer that you are working to improve yourself. For the immediacy of an upcoming interview, formulate the most positive version of your interpersonal skills. Here are a few examples of bad answers:

"I get along well with just about everybody."

"I can pretty much get along with everybody, but I don't really like it when I have to deal with a co-worker who doesn't pull their own weight (or who gossips, etc.)."

We have talked about the first answer, so let's look at the second. It seems fine, but the interviewer is only hearing *your* side of the problem. They don't know you, so they may wonder whether you are the problem in such a situation because you lack strong interpersonal skills. We all can have trouble with people, but now is not the time to draw attention to it. Consider this positive answer:

"I think it's important to make a special effort to get along with customers, management and co-workers. I try to approach every situation with an open mind. I find the best way to deal with others is to listen to their needs before saying anything. When you are dealing with an unhappy person, they may be having a bad day and need a kind word. When I worked at the XYZ Company, I was always called out to deal with complaining customers. My supervisor received a number of letters from customers complimenting my outstanding service. In fact, I have copies of some of those letters in my portfolio. Would you like to see them?"

Success-Oriented Questions
"Describe the accomplishment that you are most proud of in your career (or, for new grads, education)."

Your answer will demonstrate whether you are result- and goal-oriented, how you perceive yourself and your accomplishments, and what you value as important. Try to focus on one accomplishment that carries the greatest impact. Consider answers like these:

Work-Related:

"I'm proudest of my accomplishment as group manager for the First Annual Microsoft Certified Solutions Provider (MCSP) Conference, Fusion '06. I was responsible for developing strategy and driving content, logistics and theme for the conference, which required extensive planning, leadership of forty people in cross-functional teams, marketing, budgeting and implementation. It was a major endeavour that I undertook on six months' notice. The program was extremely well received in the industry, resulting in XXXXX attendees. Subsequent conferences have followed the entire template that I helped to develop."

School-Related:

"During my junior year as a marketing major at the University of XYZ, I competed against several seniors for an internship with the Florida Solar Energy Center. I was selected and began my 160-hour internship at the perfect time. They were in the process of preparing for the Sixth Annual Sunday Challenge, a major media event. I had the opportunity to help co-ordinate the event, including details like planning, organizing, promoting and publicizing. I contacted potential participants and sponsors, organized media folders, wrote press releases, performed preliminary research and co-ordinated with members of the marketing team. It was fulfilling and made me feel more prepared to join a marketing team when I graduated."

"If you set out to reach a goal, are you frequently successful in achieving it?"

Are you pessimistic or optimistic? Can you achieve the goals you set for yourself? Do you give up, or go for the gold? Are you a leader or a loser? There is so much riding on your answer to this question, so be ready to sell yourself and demonstrate your logical thinking. This is not the time for the failed idea or broken dream to surface.

"I've been known to set some pretty tough goals for myself, but I have also been extraordinarily successful in achieving them. I attribute this to critical planning skills, strong motivation and, most importantly, the advice of one of my early clients. She said that the main ingredient in her success was persistence with charm. She believed in never giving up until she got to yes. This strategy reminded me of the way little kids go about getting what they want. Before this insight I was always taking steps to meet my goals, but quietly in the background. My client's advice inspired me to be more dynamic in pursuing my goals. Since that day, I have met goals, including being published in eight books, speaking at a national conference and establishing my own newspaper column."

"Have you ever not pursued a goal because someone said you could not achieve it?"

This is a good question as it will show how resilient you are, how well you deal with challenges, and whether you can overcome adversity. If you have both achieved and failed to reach your goals, remember to stick to positive examples when answering. If you suddenly find yourself incapable of naming a goal you have met when someone said you couldn't, you might want to re-evaluate your relationships and any issues you have with self-trust. Consider the following:

> "When I was younger, it always seemed like it was more important to fit in and be a part of the crowd. My parents always encouraged me to achieve. They stressed the importance of planning for the future, of believing in myself and of knowing I could do anything. When I was about eleven, I wanted to play street hockey instead of doing my homework. 'Stick with your education,' my mom said. She told me that the people I admired worked and studied hard to get ahead. My parents pushed me. They tried to help with my homework, but they also encouraged me with a reward of playing hockey for a limited number of hours. I resented these limitations at the time, but now I am grateful. I feel this has been a solid basis for the success I achieve in meeting the goals I do today."

Flexibility Questions
"How do you handle deadlines and pressure?"

Are you a multi-tasker? Are you motivated? Do you crack at the first signs of pressure? Many people make a common mistake in answering this question. Read the following response and try to improve it.

> "I don't mind deadlines or pressure at all. In fact, I feel that I am at my best at these times. Knowing that I have a deadline and a goal to meet really keeps me on track."

The problem with this answer is that it demonstrates a lack of self-motivation. Even in the most mundane of jobs, employers feel they should get their money's worth for your time. They would like to believe that you are working steadily and can get the job done, and not just when you're under the gun. Consider this answer instead:

> "I don't mind deadlines or pressure. In any job, you can expect to have deadlines, last-minute requirements and even emergencies that have to be dealt with. It's a part of the job. I make a point of being organized and keeping to a schedule, rather than waiting till the last minute. That way, I can deal more effectively with any special requirements or challenges."

"Can you handle multiple tasks or projects? Give me an example of a situation where you did this successfully."

This is another key question, because the ability to handle multiple tasks is paramount in most positions. In fact, the highest cost to employers is in replacing or retraining personnel who can't meet the demands of the workplace. You may not realize it, but the positive point here is that you were asked to give an example. Now you can follow through and paint a picture of your abilities.

> "With the frequent downsizing at the XYZ Company, where I worked for six years, I handled multiple job responsibilities and projects at the same time. When I was hired, there were six territory managers in the state. One by one, territories were merged and managers were let go. I received a larger geographic territory with more clients to provide quality service to. All clerical support was cut out and managers were given laptops to handle all order processing, follow-through, reporting and communications. Although it was challenging, especially with the additional travel requirements, I consistently exceeded my productivity goals while maintaining client satisfaction."

"Describe how you would handle an unhappy customer."
Your answer demonstrates how you handle problems responsibly.

> "I believe that the greatest detriment to a company's success is an unhappy customer. One unhappy customer can ruin the reputation of an otherwise good organization. I make a point of going the extra mile not to upset a customer. When something goes wrong or I to have to deal with an unsatisfied customer, I take steps to solve the problem. I think ownership of the problem is the key. I know how frustrating it is when a customer gets passed from person to person. They just get more and more agitated. I try to handle it by listening to the customer, but if it is above my head, I seek out the appropriate manager and introduce them to the customer and the problem to make sure it is followed through."

Responsibility-Level Questions
"Describe a situation in which you were unsuccessful achieving a goal. How did you respond?"
How can you answer positively when you are being baited to answer negatively? Your answer showcases your level of maturity when responding to a challenge and lets the interviewer know what you do when you don't get your way. Consider the following positive answer:

> "I ran for president of the local chapter of the National Association of Female Executives but wasn't elected. I was disappointed, but I didn't let it get me down. Instead, I applied myself further within the organization, chairing committees and special projects. I won the next election."

"How would you describe career success?"
This is another test of your maturity level.

> "I like the quote, 'Success is a journey, not a destination.' To me, successful people consistently pursue opportunities for learning. Success

is not about being the highest-paid or having the nicest car; I believe career success is the internal satisfaction that comes from learning from each and every experience."

"What do you hope to get out of this job?"

The interviewer wants to know how realistic your expectations are. Consider this positive answer:

"Joining your company can help me further my career by expanding my skill base. I'm especially interested in becoming involved in the launch of your new firewall software. The opportunity to work with cutting-edge technology in a well-known company such as yours will put me in the forefront of product marketing and development, further honing my skills and preparing me to pursue promotions based on my advancing skills."

Now that you have some guidelines about answering interview questions, you must prepare to say your answers out loud. Enlist a friend or fellow job-seeker to take on the interviewer's role. Please note that to gain the most from this exercise, your friend will have to take their role seriously. They will need to pay attention to your answers and mannerisms in order to give you some constructive suggestions for improvement.

Here are some points to review as you practise being interviewed:

- Are you being too curt and not giving enough detail in your answers? Ensure that you take the time to communicate enough information for the interviewer to learn more about you.
- Are you rambling? Make your points without going off on tangents. Concentrate on the question. Ask for clarification before you start answering if you do not grasp what you are being asked.
- What is your body language saying about you? Do not chew your pen or fingernails, twirl your hair or tap your foot. If you are nervous, and the majority of people are, clasp your hands loosely together and keep your feet flat on the floor.

- Is your speech littered with "um," "like," "you know" and other stretchers? Take a deep breath and speak slowly and clearly.
- How do you carry yourself? Sit up straight and make eye contact.
- Do you sound too practised? You want to be prepared, but you don't want to recite your answers in a way that makes you appear stiff.
- Are you listening to the whole question? You might be tempted to start answering before the interviewer has finished asking the question. Wait and think about what you are going to say before interrupting the interviewer.

THE VIDEO PRACTICE INTERVIEW CHECKLIST

- Do I have good posture?
- Am I making eye contact with the interviewer?
- Are my answers delivered too quickly or too slowly?
- Does my tone make me seem believable?
- Am I exhibiting any distracting mannerisms?
- Do I use "umh," "ahh" or other hesitant words when delivering my answers?

A video camera is a great learning tool. Record and constructively review a mock job interview. You can learn to improve your interview skills by hearing what you say and watching how you say it. If you don't have a video camera, use a tape recorder. You will be amazed at how much you can learn about yourself and your interview strengths and weaknesses from listening to the tone of your voice and the confidence with which you deliver your answers.

If you have learned anything about the company or the people who are going to be interviewing you, how can you connect with them? Did you both go to the same university? Do you have the same books on your shelves? If there is a way to make yourself a person rather than a product, the interviewer will have a harder time turning you down for the job.

You need to know your life. You need to be able to answer the question, "So tell me about yourself," without missing a beat. You need to be able to discuss in detail each aspect of your résumé and how it might apply to the job you are pursuing. Prepare for your interview further by using this Pre-Interview Checklist.

Pre-Interview Checklist

- Read and review the interview questions in this chapter, and write out your own answers.
- Visualize yourself answering the questions. Be realistic. Determine where you want to improve and what steps you can take.
- Imagine your worst-case scenario. What is the question you are dreading being asked? Prepare yourself to be able to answer that one without skipping a beat.
- Anticipate other questions that are specific to your target industry.
- Practise your answers with a volunteer and record these sessions with a video camera or a tape recorder.
- Review your practice interview tape and devise strategies to improve your answers and your delivery. Consult the videotape or your volunteer for feedback on your body language. Consider each of the points outlined on page 152.
- Review your company research.
- Review your answers to the tough questions.
- Get directions to the place of the interview, and double-check the time, place and room.
- Select the clothes that you will wear. If you are unsure of appropriate dress, go at lunchtime to the building where you are interviewing and take note of what people are wearing.
- Review names of interviewer(s) if known.
- Place extra copies of résumés in your briefcase or portfolio.
- Gather any other resources that have been identified as useful to bring.

THE INTERVIEW PROCESS

Before you go into the interview, make sure you understand where you are in the interview process. Different types of interviews will require different strategies on your part. There are three major types of interviews: screening, selection and confirmation.

The Screening Interview

Some employers, though not all, will subject you to a screening interview. The screening interview is used to narrow down a large number of candidates. Most often these are conducted by telephone. Be prepared to explain why you want the job, and give examples linked to your résumé that demonstrate your ability to do the job. You can also use this opportunity to gather information about the company and the position so that when you get the second interview — called the selection interview — you will be even better equipped to sell yourself. At the screening stage you are not going to get the job offer, so approach it as a means to get to that important second selection interview.

Be prepared for a screening interview with:

- an articulate, thought-out reason why you want the job
- an ability to verify your résumé
- an explanation of any obvious weaknesses on your résumé
- questions for the interviewer that will help you prepare for the next interview

PHONE INTERVIEWS

The telephone is frequently used for initial interviews, and may be used if you are interviewing for a job in a different city. This type of interview is no less formal than one conducted in person, so you should be no less prepared. Except for extreme circumstances, your primary goal for a phone interview is to be selected for a face-to-face interview. Here are some strategies for phone interviews:

- Ensure that everyone in your house knows how to answer the telephone properly and take messages. If you are expecting the call, answer the phone yourself.
- Find a private space where you will not be interrupted.
- Avoid using a cordless telephone — the batteries may fail.
- Do not use a cell phone. As good as cellular networks can be, a transmission sometimes cuts out.
- Budget enough time. The majority of phone interviews take more than twenty minutes, and some have been known to go for hours. When you schedule the interview, ask approximately how long it will last. If it goes beyond that length (a good sign!) and you are unable to carry on, politely ask if you can continue the conversation later or if you can come in for a face-to-face meeting.
- Be professional. You cannot afford to be sloppy because the interview is not conducted in person. You still need to put your best foot forward.
- Make sure you have notes and a pen and paper to write down questions as they are asked. It is far easier to take notes in a phone interview than in a face-to-face one.
- Attempt to engage the interviewer. The same concept of the face-to-face interview holds here. You want the interviewer to do a meaningful portion of the talking.
- Listen mindfully. Eliminate background distractions such as TV, radio or your computer.
- Don't answer your call waiting!

Selection Interview

The selection interview is where the rubber meets the road, the place where you get to tell your story. Your ability to communicate this information will either open doors or clearly shut them; it all depends on your storytelling ability and your ability to present yourself well.

THE INTERVIEW CHECKLIST

The day before the interview:

• Lay out your clean clothes. Make sure they are pressed.

• Assemble extra résumés, lists of references, and any other materials you will take with you in a briefcase or portfolio.

• Use Mapquest or Google Maps to generate accurate directions to the building where the interview is to be held. Know the floor number, the suite number and the telephone extensions of the people with whom you are meeting.

• Get a good night's sleep.

The day of the interview:

• Shave (gentlemen), shower, and clean and cut your nails.

• Arrive ten minutes early but no earlier. If you have had a coffee, use a breath mint or brush your teeth before the interview.

• If you smoke, avoid doing so before your interview. Many employers frown on this habit, and studies have shown that if a smoker and a non-smoker are equally qualified, the non-smoker will get the job. If the topic of smoking comes up in the interview, don't lie: you will be found out eventually.

• Be mindful of your breathing. If it is quick and shallow, take a moment to calm yourself. Inhale and count in your head to five, hold your breath for the count of five, and then exhale to the count of five. Repeat five times.

• Check your hair, teeth, zipper and outfit.

• When you arrive at the interview location, always be polite to the people you meet. Some of the people you meet on your way to the interview may be members of the interview team!

• Turn off your cell phone and portable organizer before you enter.

• If your interview is at lunch or dinner, brush up on your manners. Order something that you can't spill — nothing too messy. Unless you're picking up the tab, order moderately priced items and don't overdo it.

• If the interviewer is running behind, use this lull to practise your breathing or other relaxation techniques.

When the interviewer comes out to meet you, stand up and establish eye contact, smile and shake their hand firmly. Follow them into the interview room and sit when you are offered a chair. If your interview is taking place within the interviewer's office, look around for conversation starters such as a piece of art or a photograph of your interviewer holding the fish that didn't get away.

One word of caution: some topics are off-limits. Even if your interviewer is surrounded by family photos, you don't know what might have happened since the photos were taken. Never ask, even if he or she is wearing a wedding ring, about the spouse. I once had an interview where I thought it safe to ask, "What does your wife do?" Much to my dismay, the interviewer had gotten separated that morning! Therefore, pick a topic that is timeless and relatively safe, such as where they went to university or the picture of Paris on the wall. Be careful here, too: if you see a Picasso in the office, and you say "I love Picasso" but don't have anything further to add, the conversation-starter could backfire.

The interview decision can be made within the first two minutes, so be mindful of your body language and how you present yourself. I can't stress enough how important your body language is during an interview. Whether consciously or subconsciously, it conveys your state of mind to the person you're speaking with, and interviewers are practised at noticing these details. Have you ever spoken with someone who won't look you directly in the eye? You've no doubt noticed that their communication skills seem different than those of the person who makes eye contact. You may not feel a connection with a person who is always looking at his or her feet.

Here are some tips to improve your body language during your interview:

- **Don't fidget.** Be aware of your nervous habits. Don't tap the desk, play with your hair, bite your fingernails or touch your face constantly. These will be perceived by the interviewer as indicators of a low confidence level.
- **Sit up straight.** Put both of your feet on the floor and be careful not to slouch. Lean slightly towards the interviewer.

- Don't lean on the interviewer's desk. If you do, you are invading the interviewer's personal space.
- Make eye contact throughout the course of the interview. Don't stare, just maintain comfortable and natural eye contact. If there's more than one person interviewing you, always look at the person who is talking, and when answering questions, look at each each in turn.
- Watch your hands. If you're the kind of person who likes to gesture with your hands, clasp them loosely and hold them in your lap.
- Remove barriers. Be careful not to create defensive barriers between yourself and the interviewer(s). Don't keep your arms folded or your legs crossed. It may feel natural to you, but it does set up a defensive barrier.
- Be natural. The more natural you can appear to be, the better your chance of creating a good impression. Since you practised before the interview, now you can focus on your answers more than on your mannerisms.

Let the interviewer know that you are interested in the job, that you can do the job and that you are, in fact, the best person for the job. This is your chance to set the tone of the interview, rather than have it dictated to you. The interviewer has the power to hire you or not, and he or she is under pressure not to make a hiring mistake. Employers do not want to hire someone who will not work out. It has been said that finding a good employee through the interview process is only 3 percent more probable than picking a name out of a hat, and this is assuming there is someone suitable to pick in the first place. The reality is that human resources professionals can make bad choices. Hiring is not a science, but an art.

Keep your answers crisp but not curt, and within a time frame of twenty seconds to two minutes. Every answer you provide needs to connect back to the theme of "This is why I am good for the position." Speak clearly and don't be cocky; instead, be humble, honest and self-confident. If necessary, ask to have the question repeated, especially if it is a multi-part one. In one interview, I remember being asked a three-point question that took over a minute to ask. By the end, I had no idea what the initial part of the question was. Your interviewers probably have their questions written down and can repeat or clarify them.

The interview process allows you to examine whether or not you would want to work for the companies that are interviewing you. Try to zero in on what the job will involve. If you can get the interviewer to talk about an unfinished project or an area they want to move into, give some positive suggestions. By getting an idea of where the department is headed, you will get a sense of whether you want to be part of the employee base. Let the interviewer talk. If they describe things about the company, encourage them by asking them to elaborate.

When you are being asked a question, you may want to jot down notes to keep your thoughts straight. Politicians take notes during debates to ensure their answers stay on track.

Be aware of the effect you are having on the interviewer. How are they responding to your answers? Are they leaning back? Do they look confused? If they look confused or concerned, slow down and focus on providing a confident answer. If you notice that, while you are giving an answer, they are leaning forward and seem to be interested, expand on your answer with more detail. Understanding what the other person is thinking is a difficult skill, but if you can be responsive to the interviewer's body language, you are guaranteed a more successful interview.

If a company is searching for a new employee they may have a problem. It could be a good one (for instance, how to manage growth) or a bad one (perhaps they had to let a previous employee go). Present yourself as someone who can become the solution to the problem. Make it clear that you are a problem-solver rather than someone who just keeps busy. The interview provides you with a chance to make an oral presentation on how you can do this.

The majority of employers are looking for the following traits in an employee:

- punctuality
- willingness to work overtime
- dependability
- good time-management skills
- good written and oral communication skills
- willingness to train
- an interest in lifelong learning
- flexibility
- ability to react well under pressure
- loyalty
- the ability to spot trends

The traits you exhibit should be highlighted in the interview by using examples whenever you can.

Although most interview questions are about your past, the employer wants to know how your past will predict your future. Frame your responses in a way that gives the interviewer confidence. Be positive and excited about your future. Hope is something that is lacking in this world, and if you can go into the interview hopeful, it will go a long way towards convincing the company that you have a successful future with them.

This can be a small world, and the person interviewing you could turn out to be a best friend of the lousy boss you had a few years ago. Speak graciously about previous employers, even if, deep down, you want to tell everyone you meet about how bad it was to work there.

You will notice that the questions follow a time line — they start out dealing with your distant past, then move on to the present and into the future. The more future-oriented the questions become, the better you are doing (as a rule). If the questions are rooted in the past, you should attempt to frame your answers in the future. As the questions become future-focused, you may want to ask questions of your own, such as:

- What is the specific job I am being considered for?
- If I were hired, what would my responsibilities be?

- Would I be working in a team or as an individual?
- To whom would I report?
- How much training will I need in order to get up to speed?
- What is the evaluation process?
- What were the strengths and weaknesses of the previous people who held this position? (If they had weaknesses, this as an opportunity to highlight how you are different.)
- Why did you, the interviewer(s), decide to work here?
- What do you wish you had know about the company before you started?
- What particular characteristics do you think have made you successful here?
- May I meet the people I would be working with and for (if it isn't the interviewer)?

The Company Tour

During the course of the interview, you may be taken on a tour of the company or department. This is an opportunity to meet potential teammates, and it allows the interviewers to observe you in an awkward setting. They want to see how you fit with your potential colleagues. Be friendly and polite and try to convey warmth to the people you meet.

ENDING THE INTERVIEW

When you reach the end of the interview, finish strongly. If you have additional questions, ask them now. These questions may be prepared before the interview. Most interviewers do not mind if you ask a few questions; just make sure they have not answered them earlier in the interview. If the interview is running long, you can offer to send the interviewer your questions by e-mail. Whatever you do, don't say that you have no questions. This is a last opportunity to sell yourself.

However, first assess the situation to determine how aggressive you can be in the end-of-interview questions. If the interview has gone longer than scheduled, you have been asked to submit references, or they start asking specific questions about when you can start working and other practical issues, this is a strong sign that you can be more forthright in your pursuit of the job.

Questions you may want to ask at the end of an interview include:

- Given my skills and experience, is there work that I could be considered for in your company? (If this is an interview that is not about a specific job.)
- Would you like me to come back for another interview, perhaps with some of the other decision-makers? (If you can secure a second interview, it has been a successful first interview.)
- When may I expect to hear from you? If they answer with "We need to think about this," you need to follow up by asking "Might I ask what would be the latest date I might hear from you?" Then ask, "May I contact you after that date, if for any reason you haven't gotten back to me by that time?"

If the questions above have been answered in the negative, you might ask if the interviewer can think of anyone else who might be hiring for a position you'd be well-suited for. This takes confidence, but keep in mind that although you may not have succeeded in this interview, you may be the perfect candidate for another job.

Last but not least, ask for the job. People rarely do this because it seems forward. It *is*, but it demonstrates enthusiasm and self-confidence. You can say, "I am very interested in this job; do you have any reservations about choosing me to fill the position? If you do, I'd like the chance to clear them up right now." You just might get the job and not have to worry about follow-up. Inquire about the next steps in the process and ask when you might expect to hear something. Thank the interviewer at the end of the meeting.

Knowing how to close an interview properly is difficult for most of us. If you feel that the company is one you would want to work for, say so near the end of the interview. Showing interest makes it clear that you're serious about the opportunity. You can say something like,

"I'm really impressed with your company, your products/services, and everyone that I've had the opportunity to meet. I'm confident that I could do a great job in the position that we've discussed." Don't hesitate to reiterate your interest in the company by asking about the next step in the process. If you get the impression that the particular job you've interviewed for isn't a great fit, stay upbeat, because there may be another opportunity in the company for which you'd be a better fit. If you've left a good impression with the hiring manager, they may consider you for another position or refer you to someone else who could hire you. Remember to be enthusiastic. The more people you make a good impression on during your job search, the better. An interviewer can become a valuable networking source even if you don't get the job.

After the Interview

Small talk sometimes ensues after the interview process. Don't breathe a sigh of relief and divulge how nervous you were. If personal questions come up in the informal setting, you must still answer confidently. You may expand on parts of the interview that went well or on the information you gained that has excited you about working for the company.

If you are currently employed and interviewing for a new job, talk positively about your current job, if asked, and say polite things about your boss. Remember what your mother probably told you — if you can't say something nice about someone, don't say anything at all. The hiring manager knows you are leaving your current job because you aren't completely happy, so don't dwell on it. In the post-interview chat, ask questions to learn more about the company. If the interviewer starts complaining or gossiping, this might not be the best company to work for.

Lastly, remember those thank-you cards I keep talking about? When you get home, write one, stamp it and get it in the mail by the next morning. Don't forget this critical step.

DEALING WITH CHALLENGING INTERVIEW SITUATIONS

There are times when an interview will present challenges you could not have forseen. Here are some of the most common examples.

The incompetent interviewer. They have no clue what they are doing; they may leave your résumé behind or come to the interview without any idea of the hiring criteria. If you can control the interview, you can use this situation to your advantage; if you lose control, you will have a very tough time. These situations are better for people with obvious qualifications. Incompetent interviewers need to be led — lead them towards offering you the job.

The rambler. These interviewers like to talk and are thrilled to meet a new face who hasn't heard all of their stories. As I have mentioned before, this is not necessarily a bad thing. Getting the interviewer talking is important; however, you need to be sure to have the opportunity to present your case for getting the job. Don't prevent them from talking, but choose appropriate moments to sell yourself. Ask clear questions about the job you are going after.

Emotionless people. Some interviewers deliberately approach the interview as an opportunity to intimidate you. This may raise alarms about why you would want to work for this company. The best advice is not to let yourself be thrown off. If you don't get positive feedback, don't worry about it — and don't waste your time trying to figure out what the person is thinking. Present your case, ask your questions and finish the interview.

The trickster. These people view the interview process as a game designed to trip you up. If they succeed, handle it with grace. Show them that you are unflappable. If the situation is bordering on becoming out of hand, however, you need to make it clear that the direction of the interview concerns you and that you would prefer to focus on the job at hand and your qualifications for it.

The late interviewer. Interviewers sometimes run late. This is never a good situation, because the interviewer may end up giving you less than their full attention. If the interview still hasn't begun thirty minutes after the scheduled time and you haven't been given a reason, inquire as to whether it can be rescheduled. This can serve as an example of your calmness and ability to deal with frustrating situations.

Group interviews. These interviews are difficult because you may find yourself up against a variety of interview styles. There are some benefits to group interviews, however — chief among them, you get the chance to demonstrate that you can communicate within a group. Group dynamics are key, especially if the job you are applying for is performed in a team context. Here are some things to keep in mind during the group interview:

- Respond to each member of the group on an individual basis. Learn the names of the interviewers and direct your answers back to the one who asked the question, not to the group.
- Don't ignore people. If there are particular interviewers who are doing most of the talking, don't forget the others. The dominant interviewers may not be the people with the primary power to hire you. Move your gaze from person to person, and be sure to make eye contact with each.
- Stick to your strategy. It is more difficult within a group, but not impossible.

Illegal questions. You cannot be asked questions about your religion, age, ethnic origins, race or marital status. If an interviewer tries to ask such a question, ask tactfully whether the information has a direct bearing on the job responsibilities. If they give a good reason, then answer the question. If they don't and press you to answer, state that you are not comfortable discussing personal subjects that are unrelated to the job.

Pre-employment testing. If, in the course of the interview, you are asked to take a test, don't panic, even if you haven't prepared. These tests may range from the wacky (handwriting tests) to the practical (a test of whether you understand the basics of the company's industry). They may include personality, psychological, physical and aptitude tests. It is also becoming more commonplace to administer drug tests. If you are asked to take a drug test, detail the medications and foods you consume that may cause a false test. For example, poppy seeds, while innocuous, can generate a false positive result for opium.

THE POST-INTERVIEW SELF-EVALUATION

After you have gone home and sent the thank-you card, take thirty minutes to assess your performance. Ask yourself the questions below. Then use the Post-Interview Evaluation form that follows to help you record important details.

- What points did I make that seemed to interest the interviewer?
- Did I present myself in the best possible light?
- How did I handle the questions/situations designed to throw me off my game?
- Did I clearly explain my goals, interests and desires in relation to the job at hand?
- Did I miss opportunities to highlight my abilities or talents and how they relate to the organization?
- Did I talk too much? Too little?
- Was I tense? Fidgety?
- Did my initial attempt at connecting with the employer work? Why or why not?
- Did I learn enough about the job to make an informed decision and assessment about its fit with my right job criteria?
- What can I do better in my next interview?

POST-INTERVIEW EVALUATION FORM
Position interviewed for:
Interviewed by:
Length of interview:
Type of interview:
Questions asked by interviewer:
Concerns regarding the position:
Would I leave my current situation for this opportunity?
Rate this opportunity out of 10, and state reasoning:
What would increase its ranking?
Opinions of family/friends regarding this opportunity:
Do I want this job?

Callbacks and Confirmation Interviews

In many cases, the hiring process involves several interviews. You may be called back to meet different people. If this is the case, stick to the guidelines covered in this chapter; if they worked the first time, they should work again. Subsequent interviews may be the preface to a job offer, as with the confirmation interview, and salary negotiations. The confirmation interview is, in most cases, a rubber-stamp process, and should be taken as a sign that you have the job. But don't be cocky or complacent! Be on your best behaviour and take nothing for granted.

UNFORTUNATELY...

Consider this scenario: in the end it has come down to a choice between you and another individual; the call comes, and it begins, "I'm sorry to inform you..." Your first reaction may be to lash back, but that is the worst possible thing you could do. Respond graciously: "Thank you so much for the opportunity, and for taking the time to let me know personally." Don't start an argument or create additional awkwardness by asking why you didn't get the job. Rather, ask what particular strengths gave the edge to the candidate who got the offer. Read between the lines, and you can use the information to improve your chances at the next job.

Before the conversation ends, let the hiring manager know that you would be interested in any future opportunities at the company, or that you'd love to get a call if it doesn't work out with the number one candidate. You might leave the manager second-guessing him or herself. Alternatively, you may be "wait-listed," which means that you weren't the right person for the current job, but you may be a perfect fit for a recently vacated job in another department.

IT'S NOT YOU, IT'S THE PROCESS

Sometimes the reason you don't get the job may be beyond your control. Many companies, particularly mid-sized to large organizations, have a process to follow before they hire. Here are some common issues that may come into play.

The internal candidate. The company has to justify its hiring decision and looks outside only to justify that a "thorough" search has been undertaken. You may have been a reference point to defend the decision to hire or promote from within.

Reorganization. The company started the hiring process before a decision was made at a higher level to restructure. This often results in changes to the leadership as well as the type of person they are looking for (if they are still looking for anyone at all.)

Job description skew. As the hiring manager starts the process of interviewing, he or she realizes the role has been defined incorrectly. This may also happen once the interview process is under way — the very act of talking to candidates has caused the manager to revisit the sorts of problems and opportunities he or she is really facing.

Budgets. A project may lose its funding, or another initiative may have taken a higher priority in terms of time, money and personnel, so the hiring needs for the department are now different.

"X" factors. Wild and crazy things do happen, ranging from personal to organizational crises, that put the kibosh on the need to hire.

Don't lose hope. A lot can happen in the first two months of a job. Make sure you still send thank-you notes to everyone involved in the process. These will be hard notes to write, but it is an important task to complete because it will prove that you are a classy candidate. You will strengthen the relationships rather than end them. And make sure the people you have dealt with are added to your network list.

SALARY NEGOTIATIONS

If you make it to the negotiating stage, congratulations! This is the goal that all job-seekers aspire to. Now that you have secured the job you dreamt about, it is time to obtain the salary you deserve to accommodate the lifestyle you've envisioned for yourself.

Negotiating is difficult. You should have a strong sense of several factors — your acceptable salary range, your desired title and your expected level of responsibility — before you even get to the interview. Of course, the employer may have an equally firm idea of what the company wants to pay you. Negotiation is always a process of give and take. If you adhere to the following techniques, you should succeed in getting a salary you deserve.

First of all, never discuss salary requirements until you reach the end of the interview process. Of course, it can be tough to pinpoint when that is. Until you are confident that you have secured the position, we recommend that you do your best to defer the discussion. There are many techniques for doing this. For instance, if the employer seems like a fair person, say, "Until you have been able to get to know me and decide that you want to hire me, and I've decided that I can add to your organization, I feel that a discussion of salary is premature." This should usually work.

However, the occasional employer will not be put off so easily. They'll want to know whether they can afford you. If you are pressured, try responding, "I'll gladly discuss salary expectations once I have a better understanding of what the job requires." Knowledge is power, so do your best not to be the first one to mention a figure. Instead, try to get the interviewer to tip his or her hand. A good approach is to say, "You have created the position and likely have a figure in mind that fits with the known responsibilities and requirements of the job. I would be interested in knowing what that figure is, or at least what range it falls within."

In some situations, no matter how hard you try to delay a discussion of salary, you won't succeed. Indeed, you may get the impression that the interviewer thinks you are playing games. If so, offer a broad salary range. If you are still pressured to come up with a specific figure, be aware that this is the way the company operates and no negotiation will be possible. This may cause you to rethink whether you want to work there.

Do not discuss salary until the following conditions have been met:

- You have decided you want to work there.
- You understand what the job involves.
- You've gotten to know your employers as much as possible.
- Your employers have gotten to know you and understand that your capabilities set you above the other applicants.

Let's assume now that you have succeeded in stickhandling your way past this potential trap and have proceeded to the negotiating stage. Preparation is as important as ever. While you weren't about to divulge a figure earlier, you should have a minimum salary requirement in mind. And you should find out as much as you can about what is reasonable to expect. Conduct research to learn what people in your field — and, if possible, within the organization — earn. (This type of information isn't always readily available but the extra work could pay off.) If the person above you earns $100K a year and the person below you earns $80K, you should go to the interview with a range of $90-$95K in mind.

You must be able to back up your salary request with reasons. "Just because" won't work here; you need a well-thought-out rationale for your expectations. And be honest with yourself about the position you are in: unless you have been hand-picked for the job, you need to realize that you probably want the job more than the company wants you. You may find it necessary to make some compromises to get in the door. Be adaptable. Negotiations are dynamic processes; you never know how they are going to turn out, and you need to go with the flow. Pay particular attention to subtle, implicit details such as body language. Bear in mind that a tough boss might want to win the first few points in order to establish a position; if you happen to know this, it would be wise to try to address the points that you are more flexible on first. And keep moving forward: don't revisit points that have already been agreed upon. Once you and the employer have a meeting of the minds on a point, make a note of it and move on.

Negotiations aren't finished until you have discussed fringe benefits (holidays, insurance, pension). These benefits can add between 15 and 30 percent to the value of your compensation. You should also discuss the employer's policy about future raises. Finally, it is imperative that you get the terms summarized in writing — request a letter of agreement or an employment contract. Document the results of the negotiations so you can double-check them when the contract arrives in the mail.

At the end of the negotiations you will be under pressure to commit. The best advice is to take a day and consider your options.

ASSESSING THE TARGET

The finish line is in view. The ultimate reward for all your hard work up to this point — the job of your dreams — is within your grasp. What do you do if you have more than one offer on the table? How do you go about choosing the best offer for you?

Childhood stories are simple and engaging, and they contain important lessons. One classic in particular, *Goldilocks and the Three Bears*, holds lessons for job seekers. Remember how the Papa Bear's bowl of porridge was too hot, while the Mama Bear's was too cold and the Baby Bear's was "just right"? We can apply this "Goldilocks Principle" to career planning. Good timing is as essential to job satisfaction as finding the right job. Too often people come across an opportunity that is "too hot" and they get burned. The job may be everything they have hoped for, but the timing is off, making it unpleasant. At other times, individuals come across an opportunity but are cautious about approaching it. They are unsure of themselves, or are afraid to take the next step. Their apprehension has let the opportunity "get cold" and it passes them by.

So, how do you know if the opportunity is "just right" — and indeed, what exactly *is* "just right"? Our taste buds are different, after all. Just because someone else was ready for a promotion or an increase in his or her work responsibility doesn't mean that you are. It doesn't matter that your brother was making x dollars when he was your age. You have to gain an understanding of your fears, your life circumstances and your family situation and make your own timelines. Along with good timing, the job that is "just right" has to fit you. You have to feel comfortable where you work, and comfort comes from a user-friendly workspace, good dynamics between co-workers, and sufficient challenges and solutions.

Opportunity Evaluation

Use the Opportunity Evaluation Worksheet that follows for every offer you are considering. This detailed worksheet covers most, if not all, of the aspects that you need to weigh before making a decision.

OPPORTUNITY EVALUATION WORKSHEET

Title:
Role:
Reporting Structure:
Department or Area:
Company:
Boss(es):
Administrative Assistant:
Other Notes:
Salary:
Bonuses:
Pension:
RRSP Contributions:
Stock Options:
Parachute Clause:
Amount of Travel:
Vacation:
Allowances (car, health club, etc.):
Medical Benefits:
Dental Benefits:
Hours:
Responsibilities:
Equipment Provided:
Other Notes:
Family or Spousal Concerns:
Are there any other offers in play? (If so, rank them.)
Have you resigned from your current job?
Has the employer agreed verbally (and in writing, if possible) to the terms and conditions of the offer?

Now that you have reviewed the job offers, don't settle for just anything. You have worked very hard to find your ideal job. Don't sacrifice all that hard work by accepting an offer too soon. There may be details in the job offer that you can negotiate.

If you are entertaining multiple offers and have eliminated some of them, it's important that you contact the companies whose offers you'll be rejecting right away. Making it to the offer stage with any company represents a significant investment of time, not only for you, but for the hiring managers as well. Failure to inform them of your decision is considered to be unprofessional, and it will leave a bad impression. Maintaining strong professional relationships is essential for anyone in the job market. The appropriate course is to send a letter or e-mail to the company immediately, letting them know that you won't be accepting their offer. Indicate that it was a difficult decision and that you have given it serious thought. Thank the employer for his or her consideration and time, as well as for the offer itself. You don't have to indicate which offer you accepted, but it's not wrong to tell them. You can also wish them well in their search for the right candidate.

RESIGNING GRACEFULLY

Making the transition to a new job or career isn't always a smooth and straightforward process. Although you're probably anxious and excited about starting your new position, there's an etiquette to be followed. If you take only one thing away from this book, let it be that you should *never* burn your bridges with the employer that you're leaving. You can't predict when or where you might encounter them again. When you resign, follow company rules and be pleasant and professional throughout the entire process. Here are some tips that will ensure that you leave a good impression:

Notice. Give plenty of notice to your manager or supervisor when you're leaving. The industry standard is two weeks, but you should double-check to determine whether your workplace's policy calls for more.

Replacement. Offer to help your manager/supervisor find your replacement. You understand better than anyone what the position requires, and you may be able to refer a good candidate or offer insight into the hiring of a competent person.

Training. Spend time with your replacement to get them up to speed so they can successfully and confidently take over for you.

Keep working. Unless you are notified otherwise, continue to work until your last day. Remain positive and contribute to your team and to your organization.

Closure. Don't leave things dangling in mid-sentence. Before you go, leave detailed progress reports outlining the status of each project you are involved in.

Departure. Before you leave, make sure that you have the contact information for key people in the company whom you'd like to keep in your network.

You should always resign in writing. Keep your letter short, professional and to the point. Indicate your intention to leave, your last day, and thank your managers for the opportunity to work with them. You can include your reason for leaving, but it's not necessary. Refer to the sample resignation letter that follows.

Sample Resignation Letter

Name
Address
City, Province Postal Code
Phone Number • E-mail Address

Date

Employer's Name
Title
Organization
Address
City, Province Postal Code

Dear Mr. / Ms. Last Name:

(The first paragraph of your letter should state that you are resigning and give the date when your resignation is effective.)

Please accept this letter as formal notification that I will be resigning from my position at XYZ Industries effective January 3, 2007.

(The next section of your resignation letter (optional) should thank your employer for the opportunities you have had during your employment with the company.)

Thank you for the opportunities you have provided me during my time with your company.

(Optional: Conclude your resignation letter by offering to assist with the transition.)

If I can be of any assistance during this transition, please let me know.

Respectfully yours,

Handwritten Signature
Typed Signature

Following the tips on the previous pages will alleviate much of the anxiety and confusion that comes from making a career transition. Although resigning isn't easy, focus on staying positive and maintaining the relationships that you've built throughout your time with the company.

CHAPTER SEVEN

HAVE A JOY-FILLED FIRST NINETY DAYS IN YOUR NEW JOB

Without a doubt, your first day at your new job will be an exciting, yet stressful, experience. Will you fit in? Will you learn quickly? Will your boss be pleased with your work? Will you see eye to eye with him or her? There used to be time to acclimatize to your new surroundings, but today, time is tight and competition is heated. New employees have a shorter honeymoon period, so you will need a plan to make the most of it.

BEFORE YOU ARRIVE

If you are moving to a new city, contact a real estate agent as soon as possible to arrange housing. Many large companies can help you relocate; ask for their expertise. Consider location, commuting distance, property amenities and population demographics when you choose your new home.

Be aware also of what you can afford. Create a new budget using the New Job Budget Planner below.

NEW JOB BUDGET PLANNER
Net Income from Job:
Net Income of Partner/Spouse:
Other Income Sources:
Total Monthly Income:

Household Expenses
Mortgage Payments/Rent:
Maintenance Costs:
Utilities:
Groceries:
Telephone (local):
Telephone (long-distance):
Internet:
Travel Expenses
Car Payments:
Car Insurance:
Commuting/Public Transit:
Taxi:
Gas:
Insurance/Medical Expenses
Health Insurance:
Life Insurance:
Disability Insurance:
Prescriptions/Services:
Financial Expenses
Credit Card Payments:
Student Loans/Other Debt:
Bank Charges:
Tuition Fees:
Child Care:
Child School Activities:
Discretionary Expenses
Cable:
Cell Phone:
Entertainment:
Hobbies:
Travel/Vacation:

Books/Magazines:	
Newspaper Delivery/Subscriptions:	
Hair Care/Personal Hygiene:	
Additional Pharmacy:	
Clothing/Shoes:	
Dry Cleaning:	
Other:	
Household Emergencies:	
Cleaning (service/supplies):	
Pets:	
Total Monthly Expenses:	
Total Budget Surplus/Deficit (Monthly Income – Monthly Expenses):	

Another pre-arrival task is to ensure that you have enough work-appropriate clothing to get through a week at your new job. Many firms have casual dress codes, but you need to be aware of what and what not to wear. The image you project initially will serve you for the entirety of your time at the company, so dress with style and flair. First impressions are lasting.

Other tasks you need to complete prior to arriving on your first day include filling out all the necessary paperwork (you want to get paid, after all) and finding out exactly when, where and to whom you report on your first day of work. Review your already-extensive notes on the company to brush up on their current status. Give yourself ample time to get to work; don't be late on the first day!

On the Job

You may have been salesperson of the year at your last company, but don't expect the red carpet to be rolled out for you at the new job. The best way to impress your peers during the first few weeks is to show interest in the company's corporate culture. Move beyond the comfort of your cubicle and get to know the people you will be working with. Be aware of who they are: what do they like to do outside of work? Make an effort to schedule a few lunches a week to interact with co-workers. Don't go on about yourself; take this time to listen to others and find any common ground. Once you have made that initial surface-level connection with your new team-mates, building a deeper working relationship with them will be that much easier.

The most important relationship you will develop on the job is the one with your supervisor. This will be different from your relationship with your co-workers. Your supervisor controls a great deal of what can happen in your first year. If you come into the organization with a willing attitude, demonstrate poise and maturity and work well with others, you may be chosen for better assignments.

Your supervisor needs to feel confident that you are going to defend his or her interests, that you are an ally as opposed to an adversary. You need to make the supervisor look good by doing quality work and completing it on time, acting like a professional and maintaining a positive attitude. One thing to watch out for: as you develop a relationship with your supervisor, avoid the "buddy" relationship; keep your personal life and your career separate.

In the workforce, there are supervisors with poor skills who can be demanding, rude and unreasonable. You can't change them. You can only change yourself and adapt to the situation. Try to focus on your supervisor's positive qualities. You are stuck with them for now, so you are best advised to use this time as an experience that will better prepare you for the relationship with your next supervisor.

DIANE FRANCIS: HOW TO WRITE YOUR OWN STORY

"All of this [career] stuff just happened; it wasn't the goal. I want to enjoy ideas, the debate of ideas, and be involved in a piece of the conversation that really matters. I don't have to dominate the conversation or lead it: I couldn't do it. It is the ride I enjoy."

Diane has had twelve different careers. She grew up in Chicago before moving to Toronto, and now she commutes between Canada and the United States as part of a very busy schedule that includes working as a columnist for the *New York Sun* and the *National Post* as well as writing books, advising start-ups and juggling speaking engagements and her own online writing.

Diane dropped out of university to get married young. She became a legal secretary. Then she and her husband decided to move to Toronto and, when they couldn't find good jobs, decided to start up their own graphic design and typesetting business. Diane had children and stayed home with them, but she grew restless. She began to get involved in political activism, from running ratepayer groups to political campaigns. She discovered that the ability to truly influence events is limited in the world of politics, so she moved to journalism, which promised a convergence of words, politics and influence.

Diane had always been a very good writer, having won numerous awards in her youth. So, at twenty-nine, she took a once-a-week writing course at Sheridan College while her children were in daycare. "I loved it and it loved me, and my teacher thought that I was very talented." Her teacher set her up with an internship at a small paper in Brampton, Ontario.

On her third day on the job, she was offered a full-time position; she covered all the issues that community newspaper columnists do, including politics, school boards and sports. "You get to see all the fires [hot issues]. I loved every minute of it. It was also great that I could work from home." This advantage enabled her to better balance her role as mother and reporter.

Fifteen months later, she started to freelance and quickly became one of the busiest, most sought-after writers for magazines, including *Maclean's*, *Chatelaine*, *The Economist* and *Canadian Business*. Later, the *Toronto Star* approached her to write about business. And from there came radio and television appearances, the first of eight books, and a triple contract with the *Toronto Sun*, *Financial Post* and *Maclean's*. She was appointed a director of the company when the *Financial Post* went daily, and in 1990 she became the editor of the paper, a task she describes as "a rocket ride and tons of fun."

Her career journey wasn't carefully planned; it grew out of her interests and passions. "I want to enjoy ideas, the debate of ideas, and be involved in a piece of the conversation that really matters. I don't have to dominate the conversation or lead it: I couldn't do it. It is the ride I enjoy." Consistent throughout her multiple careers are her principles: *You are only as successful as your ability to deal with failure*. Everyone experiences failure. Whether it is a poor test result in high school, not getting into the university of your choice or your business going under. How do you deal with a broken marriage or business setbacks? You cannot shelter children or employees — or yourself — from failure. How do you deal with nasty people or professional problems? You cannot shelter anyone completely from pain. Here are some of Diane's tips:

Take risks. Business in North America is set up to take risks and chances. This is different from Asia or Europe, where it is difficult both to a launch new business and to recover from failure if it should occur. We are in the land of "can do" opportunity.

Don't get bored. "If you get bored, it will show up in the quality of your work. I felt that if I was bored, the readers would know it and they would eventually look for other people to read." In 2005, Diane pursued a fellowship at the Joan Shorenstein Center on the Press, Politics and Public Policy at Harvard University. Interviewing more than thirty professors at Harvard helped to tune her up and get to know the players and "I came to know what I didn't know."

Location matters. It's all about the right exposure. "If you want to make it in any arena, you need to be close to where the cluster of people is — and that's also where the action is. For the Canadian media, this is Toronto; in the United States, New York. From money management to opera and ballet, it is the cluster that's important. Even though you have technology, you have to establish a personal, physical chemistry. Professional and personal support groups are important. It is an infrastructure that you need."

Be honest, work hard and have a strong, clear moral compass. "Life has taught me to be more honest. I am rigid on those tenets. It leads you to better deal with failure. You don't lose focus. This is critical in politics and policy. Be transparent. Everyone has their 'clothes off.' You'd better make sure you are not hiding anything, otherwise the world will see it."

Get Feedback!

Make sure your boss is aware of what you are working on. Ask him or her what is expected of you. Without assertiveness and persistence, you may be unnoticed until it's too late. Schedule a meeting with your boss to find out what your responsibilities and limits are. Make a concerted effort to understand his or her needs and strive to meet them effectively. Don't forget to stress your desire for constructive feedback. An open relationship with a constant communication flow is essential in building a strong bond. Your new boss will respect you all the more for taking action and being proactive. After all, a job well done by you reflects well on your boss.

Treat all employees in the organization — and not just your co-workers — with respect. Work on building rapport, especially with your supervisor's administrative assistant, because having a good relationship with him or her may help you get that important meeting with the supervisor when the schedule is otherwise booked solid. An administrative assistant who has a positive opinion of you might also share his or her fount of knowledge with you.

WHAT'S NEXT?

After a month, you should be fairly confident in your new role. At six weeks, you'll have a firm grasp of what is expected of you. Make sure that you're acting on that, and make sure your boss has seen enough of your production that he or she is confident in your ability to do the job. You may find during this period that the position initially presented to you does not match what you're actually doing. If this is the case, sit down and write a new job description. Get a list together of your most pressing deadlines, top projects and new responsibilities. You might also want to take this opportunity to explore any new areas of interest that you have identified along the way. Guide your own future within the company: take the initiative and make it known where your interests lie. If you're successful in completing the tasks assigned to you, there is no reason to think that special projects will be discouraged. Besides, creativity is what innovative business is founded on.

At the same time, be cautious in choosing your projects. Make sure they're all well thought out and that they make sense. Your objective is not to prove that you can get something done, but to prove that you can get the *right* things done. There's nothing worse than doing a lot of work only to find out that the direction in which you took the project was wrong. Have vision, but choose your work wisely.

Avoid getting into a work rut after a few months. Treat the second two months like you did the first two. Renew yourself and refocus on your tasks — get excited about them again. Try to keep things fresh and new. Whether you decide to stay in your current position or move to a new one, treat every three-month cycle as you would the first ninety days. Here are some keys to starting the job off on the right foot:

Come fresh. If possible, take at least a week off between jobs, which will allow you to relax, unwind and be ready for your first day at work.

Accept the new paradigm. Don't expect things to be the same as they were in your last job. Come with an open mind and embrace the challenge of relearning the ropes.

Understand your job. As soon as possible, meet with your boss and make sure you are both on the same wavelength. Important questions include "What are the immediate priorities and tasks that I need to address?" and "On what basis will my job performance be evaluated?"

Identify the big players. Find out who are the best salespeople, top designers, most dynamic managers. Watch how they work and emulate how they approach the job.

Be culturally intelligent. Spend a good portion of your time observing the workplace. Be aware of unwritten rules that govern behaviour. Be aware of the dress code, how long lunch is, and what people do for lunch…. Try to adapt.

Don't be an instrument of change. Unless you were hired specifically to rock the boat, wait a month or two before you try to change the workplace. Understanding the current situation is the key to changing the future.

Be discreet about your salary. Don't tell anyone what you earn.

Be a techno genius. Get up to speed on the software used in your company quickly.

Stand on guard. Just because you finally got a job does not mean it will work out. Be prepared for the worst, but expect the best. Stay in touch with recruiters, keep your network of contacts active and be aware of when you might have to move on next.

Finding the right job is a complex and lifelong journey. As you embark upon the next stage, I hope that the tools and ideas in this book provide you with a healthy balance of wisdom and practical advice. The stories that you have read are real-life examples to show you that it *is* possible to find work that is both engaging and meaningful. The people in the stories took responsibility for their working lives; they either seized or created opportunities for career satisfaction. To me, they are the heroes in this book — when all is said and done, they *made* the right job happen. And their choices have influenced and motivated Canadians, whether by providing employment to hundreds, as Leonard Lee of Lee Valley Tools does, or by inspiring a nation to believe in themselves, as Paul Henderson continues to do. Each person in this book has found their "right job," and as a result, our nation is a better place to live.

Now, as we reach the end of this book, I hope you find yourself at a new beginning — not just at the beginning of the job you were always looking for, but at the beginning of a journey that will inspire your family and your community and make Canada a better place. Please visit my website, www.rightjob.ca, and add your story to the other success stories on the site, to show others how you found the right path.

RÉSUMÉ MAKEOVERS

PROFESSIONAL RÉSUMÉ: BEFORE

JANE DOE
123 Anywhere Drive
Nelson, BC K1A 7M2
(555) 555-5188 • jdoe@anyisp.com

Career Profile

Over 12 years' experience spearheading successful corporate events and trade show programs, specifically within the corporate and agency sectors. Great skills in marketing/sales, business development, strategic planning and project management. Good at delivering return on investment through negotiations, leadership and strong interpersonal skills, including attention to detail. Successful in creating and leading core project teams, completing projects on time and within budget.

Selected Accomplishments

Successfully managed and executed an annual national trade show, travelling to 8 cities across Canada.

Presented the concept and subsequently managed the development, overall content and launch of the first internal event website for Company X, culminating in the streamlining of communication and registration processes for Company X employees and the vendor community.

Successfully launched and managed a new event management company, in Alberta, for an existing promotions company, obtaining three corporate clients and their subsequent events within the first three months.

Researched, wrote and managed the Consumer Trade Show Strategy for Company X, which was adopted by Company X Consumer as a tactical means of achieving business-plan objectives.
Recruited, trained and managed a superior trade show sales team whose efforts contributed to more than $200,000 in recurring revenues within the first three years.

Developed the first lead-driven database for Company X within the Consumer Marketing business units.

Areas of Expertise

- strategic planning and project development
- project management, including budget management, critical path, timeline, work-back and production schedules and on-site execution
- leadership and staff management
- supplier and third-party management

Business Experience

Company X, Markham, ON — Account Director
Mar. 2005 – Current
- manage client relationships and specific programs for Company X
- managed and executed the National Contractor Services Trade Show program
- managed the registration and information website, including overall development and ongoing maintenance
- budget management
- sponsor communication and relationship management
- supplier management
- manage onsite execution in 12 cities in 6 weeks
- project reconciliation

Company X, Markham, ON — Event Project Manager
Oct. 2004 – Mar. 2005
Planned and executed a series of events celebrating Company X's first anniversary in business, including:
- press conference
- black-tie gala for employees, key customers and VIPs
- first annual beach cleanup initiative
- launched the wireless handheld communications device to the business community

Company X, Belleville, ON — Event Director
Sept. 2003 – Oct. 2004
Launched a new event-management company, which included the following initiatives:

- business plan development
- marketing communications
- sales and promotions activities
- client relationship and event management and execution

Company X, Halifax, NS — Project Manager, Corporate Events
Dec. 2001 – Jan. 2003
Managed and executed corporate events, including:
- Annual General Meeting
- "Partners in Performance" Seminar Series
- "State of the Union" (President's address road show to Company X's employees)
- National Convention

Company X, Edmonton, AB — Manager, Sponsorship and Special Events
July 1981 – May 2001
A team member contributing to the management of sponsor relationships and the execution of event marketing initiatives.
- Managed and executed the Company X Ontario Consumer Trade Show Program (1989–1995)
- Manager, Operator Services Central Administration Group (1987–1989)
- Manager, Operator Services Directory Assistance (1985–1987)
- Operator (1981–1985)

References available upon request.

PROFESSIONAL RÉSUMÉ: AFTER

JANE DOE
123 Anywhere Drive
Nelson, BC K1A 7M2
(555) 555-5188 • jdoe@anyisp.com

Senior Management Professional

Dynamic Senior Manager with over 12 years' experience spearheading successful corporate events and trade show programs, specifically within the corporate and agency sectors. Exemplary skills in marketing/sales, business development, strategic planning and project management. Expert at delivering exceptional return on investment through effective negotiations, leadership and strong interpersonal skills, including attention to detail. Successful in creating and leading core project teams, completing projects on time and within budget.

- Strategic Planning & Development
- Strong Leadership & Staff Management
- Project & Budget Management
- Supplier & Third-Party Management
- Critical Problem-Solving & Analysis
- Relationship Management

Excellence in Managing People, Projects & Processes

PROFESSIONAL EXPERIENCE

COMPANY X, Markham, ON
Account Director 2005–Present
Responsibilities include managing and executing annual national trade show involving 8 cities across Canada, strengthening contractor relationships, enhancing vendor relationships with customers and maximizing efficiencies and improvements through program logistics and cost-saving opportunities, selling more booth spaces than the previous year to increase the attendance year over year and flawlessly managing and executing the shows on site.
- Increased credibility by successfully managing client relationships, managing logistics for trade show, including registration, website content, budget management, supplier management and project reconciliation.
- Enhanced vendor relationships with customers through increased involvement and product knowledge, ultimately growing loyalty and driving sales.

COMPANY X, Markham, ON
Event Project Manager   2004–2005
Responsibilities included developing and presenting creative concepts and themes, co-ordinating message via marketing communications, liaising with press and media and overall project management, including execution.
- Contributed to company success by creating and launching the concept/theme for the wireless handheld communications device to the business community, which included integrating local artisans, the business community and using Company X employees as ambassadors.
- Gained valuable knowledge of organization by planning and executing the celebrations of Company X's first anniversary in business, including a press conference, a black tie gala for employees, key customers and VIPs and the first annual beach cleanup initiative.

COMPANY X, Belleville, ON
Event Director   2003–2004
Responsibilities included helping expand the business, specifically in the field of Event Management. Wrote the marketing plan and strategy and followed up with the tactical execution of the launch. The goal was to launch a new event company in a highly competitive arena.
- Increased company exposure by successfully launching and managing a new event management company for an existing promotions company.
- Obtained three corporate clients and their subsequent events within the first six months by building client relationships, business plan development, marketing communications and sales, promotions activities, event management and execution.

COMPANY X, Halifax, NS
Project Manager, Corporate Events   2001–2003
Responsibilities included presenting concepts to senior management and realizing cost efficiencies through the streamlining of communications and management processes.
- Improved employee and vendor communications by establishing, launching and managing the development and content of the first internal event website.
- Successfully rolled out the event site to the vendor community for participation and registration for eligible events, resulting in the creation of a Master Vendor Database.
- Managed and executed corporate events including Annual General Meeting.

- Created incentive program for reviving employee spirit resulting in cost savings, using employees instead of hiring promotional staff.

COMPANY X, Edmonton, AB
Manager, Sponsorship and Special Events   1989–2001
Responsibilities included researching, writing and managing the Consumer Trade Show Strategy; recruiting, training and managing trade show sales team; designing and overseeing the production of a custom exhibit; and integrating various business units within Company X.

- Developed Consumer Trade Show Strategy, which was adopted by Company X marketing business units as a tactical means to achieve business plan objectives.
- Managed sales team with more than $200K in recurring sales to Company X within 2 years of sales and promotional campaigns at consumer shows.
- Delivered return on investment on trade show exhibit costs in the first year and delivered a profit to the various business units through nontraditional sales opportunities.
- Developed the first lead-driven database for Company X.

Manager, Central Administration Group   1987–1989
Responsibilities included managing the largest Operator Services office in Alberta with over 20 operators; dealing with Policy Grievances; and settling labour disputes while managing the daily operations of the office.

- Managed the only office in Alberta that was chosen to showcase the cutting-edge "Automated Operator Services Systems" (AOSS) management technology.

EDUCATION AND TRAINING
Executive Development — Moncton University   1993
Certified Trade Show Marketer —
George Brown College   2000

ASSOCIATIONS & AFFILIATIONS
Volunteer & Mentor: Covenant House   2001–2004

AWARDS
Best Exhibit and Best Presentation in
Consumer Trade Shows
in Alberta   1998–1999

TECHNICAL SKILLS
Software: Microsoft Office (Word, Excel, PowerPoint)

Key Differences

- The "Areas of Expertise" were taken out of the body of the résumé and set off at the top as bullets to show strengths.
- One to two sentences were included under each position/role to show responsibilities. In the "before" résumé, bullets were listed to show the specific duties only; in the revised version, responsibilities of the role were also included.
- "Selected Accomplishments" were taken out as a separate section and incorporated into the responsibilities/duties of each position.
- The sentence "References available upon request" was deleted. References will be listed on a separate sheet of paper, to be presented to a potential employer only when requested.

SALES RÉSUMÉ: BEFORE

STAN SYMONS
1-52B 20th St.
Ottawa, Ontario
M2E 8R9
H.: (555) 555-2961
C.: (555) 555-6776
ssymons@anyisp.com

Objective
A senior sales position with a progressive software manufacturer

Experience

Company X, Belleville, ON   Dec. 2002–May 2005
Territory Manager

- Developed and managed a major U.S. territory (Midwest and Great Lakes)
- Increased annual revenues from under $500k to over $4 million
- Cultivated new relationships with security-focused VARs and corporate resellers
- Collaborated with vendor counterparts to drive new business and penetrate target accounts
- Captured business from established competitors despite limited awareness of company in territory
- Directed participation in trade shows
- Utilized joint sales calls, seminars and presentations
- Responsible for all activity in territory — worked with little supervision

Company X is a value-added distributor of primarily security software. It is based in Ottawa and has distribution relationships with software manufacturers including NetIQ, Trend Micro and eEye Digital, and counts as customers resellers and systems integrators throughout the U.S. and Canada. Annual sales are in excess of $15 million.

May 1999–Nov. 2002
Company X, Ottawa, Ontario
Major Account Manager

- Sold security and connectivity software to systems integrators across Canada and the U.S.
- Acted as Product Champion for four vendors, co-ordinating marketing campaigns and serving as primary contact

April 1997–April 1999
Company X, Ottawa, Ontario
Sales Representative
- Sold primarily connectivity software to VARs and resellers across Canada
- Prospected for new business largely via cold calling

Education
Institute X, Ottawa, ON, 1995–1996
- Diploma — Applied Information Technology

X University, Wolfville, NS, 1983–1987
- B.A., Political Science
- Minor — Economics

Additional Information
Business Skills:
- solid negotiation skills
- superior technical sales skills
- effective written and oral communication skills
- excellent interpersonal skills
- work well within a team environment
- contract preparation and negotiation

Technical Skills — sound understanding of:
- Intrusion prevention and detection
- Vulnerability assessment
- Enterprise anti-virus
- Content filtering/anti-spam
- Security policies

Training
- Ongoing product training provided by vendors
- Fundamentals of Professional Selling, Business Institute
- Strategic Selling and Conceptual Selling
- Power Selling, Sales Force Training

SALES RÉSUMÉ: AFTER

STAN SYMONS
1-52B 20th St., Ottawa, ON, M2E 8R9
(555) 556-2961 • E-mail: ssymons@anyisp.com

SENIOR SALES
STRATEGIC OPERATIONS / EXECUTIVE LEADERSHIP

Dynamic and results-driven major account sales manager combining 8+ years sales, negotiation and organizational management. Expert in building, mentoring, motivating and working with high-performance teams. Independent, creative and critical thinker with sound judgment and decision-making competencies. Effective communicator, presenter and evaluator of information ensuring precise decision-making process. Decisive, direct and results-driven innovator and leader in corporate relationship management and performance improvement. Top record of performance in general business, strategic planning and operational management.

- Written and Oral Communication
- Team Building and Leadership
- Consumer Relations Management
- Critical Problem-Solving and Analysis
- Strategic Planning Development
- Contract Preparation and Negotiation
- Technical Sales
- Corporate Relationship Cultivation

Extensive Leadership, Strategic Sales, and Territory Management

---

PROFESSIONAL EXPERIENCE
COMPANY X, Belleville, ON   **2002–present**
Territory Manager
Responsibilities include the overall management, sales, operation and strategic planning for a major U.S. territory. Accountable on all activities including partner/vendor relationships, trade show participation, new business generation and joint sales calls for seminars and presentations.

- Increased annual revenues 800% by developing a major U.S. territory, cultivating new business relationships and evolving existing clients.
- Initiated new business and target accounts by collaborating with vendor counterparts and forging innovative mutually beneficial partnerships.

- Secured business from established competitors by focusing on current and future business needs and value-adding existing solutions through close affiliation with key manufacturing personnel.
- Improved brand recognition and market awareness by directing participation in trade shows, seminars and presentations.
- Trained active sales force and garnered team success through the replication of successful written campaigns and oral salesmanship.

COMPANY X, Ottawa, ON   **1999–2002**
Major Account Manager
- Maintained corporate relationships with new and existing business partners through keen contract preparation and negotiation and fine oral and written communication processes.
- Co-ordinated marketing campaigns as Product Champion for four major vendors by establishing significant operational strategies and issuing innovative customer care.

COMPANY X, Ottawa, ON   **1997–1999**
Sales Representative
- Sold connectivity software across Canada by focusing sales strategy on regional requirements and individual client requests.
- Prospected sufficient new business through effective telephone and e-mail communication, concentrating on superior technical knowledge and sales skills.

EDUCATION & TRAINING
Applied Information Technology — Institute   **1996**
Bachelor of Arts (Political Science, Economics) — University   **1987**
Fundamentals of Professional Selling — Business Institute   **2005**
Strategic Selling and Conceptual Selling   **2005**
Power Selling — Sales Force Training   **2005**

TECHNICAL QUALIFICATIONS
Secure Networking:
Intrusion Prevention and Detection, Vulnerability Assessment, Enterprise Anti-Virus, Content Filtering/Anti-Spam, Security Policies

Software:
Superior level of knowledge

Key Differences

- An introductory paragraph was added to show the candidate's top skills.
- The body of the résumé was reorganized and the dates were moved from the left to the right.
- The content, particularly the responsibilities, was expanded to showcase a range of skills.
- The format was streamlined to look more professional.
- A strong, catchy job title was added at the beginning of the résumé.

ENGINEERING RÉSUMÉ: BEFORE

Justin Daley, P.Eng., PMP
321 Laurier Crescent, Toronto, ON K2P 3R5
(555) 555-8288
jdaley@anyisp.com

SKILLS SUMMARY
- Problem-solving
- Project and people management
- Business planning and operation
- Written and verbal communications
- Information system analysis, design, development, testing and deployment

EXPERIENCE
April 2000–Present
Company X (www.Company X.ca)
Mississauga, ON

PROGRAM MANAGER – PROGRAM MANAGEMENT OFFICE
Led a global team of 7 senior resources in the establishment of a program management office responsible for the oversight of information systems on major engineering, procurement and construction management projects. Established standard global software support and development models. Facilitated the planning, prioritization and execution of internal projects to enhance the information systems. Created standard global commercial and licensing models. Advised the executive on issues of strategic importance.

REGIONAL DIRECTOR (NORTH AMERICA) – COMPANY X SYSTEMS
Developed business strategies with practice leaders and other regional leaders. Co-ordinated resource utilization between the different technical practices. Defined and managed the quality management system for the business unit. Planned and participated in performance appraisals/career development process.

PROJECT EXPERIENCE
Managed a project using Company X resources to deliver a custom-developed diamond management system for a client whose internal team's previous efforts were unsuccessful. State-of-the-art information system was delivered ahead of schedule and under budget.

Developed a comprehensive project work plan for 2 diamond management systems. Administered project execution by a core client team supplemented with Company X resources. Designed and executed a strategy for knowledge transfer to the client that included defining key artifacts and defining and implementing tools for long-term system maintenance.

Led a team performing a technical assessment of a system under development to identify key issues associated with project execution. Delivered a prioritized action plan to ensure a successful system implementation.

Defined system requirements and directed a team developing a database application to calculate cost estimates and operational parameters for tunnel construction and related activities. Designed and implemented systems to support project execution and software maintenance.

Proposed a plan to merge two natural gas business transaction management systems in response to a corporate merger. Managed the successful implementation of the approved plan, which was part of a larger co-ordinated effort to rationalize information systems. Played a lead role in the analysis, design and coding of changes in functionality.

Defined business, user and system requirements for a finished product quality system to be used by a global consumer packaged goods manufacturer. Developed a plan for software development and global deployment of the proposed system and estimated budgetary cost.

Led a team to analyze the current state of production systems for a consumer packaged goods manufacturer. Facilitated the definition of conceptual and logical architectures and developed a technology strategy for consideration as part of an overall corporate IT strategy.

Executed a recovery plan on a project to evaluate options for upgrading a data collection system for a consumer packaged goods manufacturer. Joined the existing project team to understand issues and advise on a course of action. Restructured project activities and roles to guarantee a successful completion.

January 2000 to March 2000
Independent Consultant
Toronto, ON

PROJECT EXPERIENCE
Analyzed, designed, developed and tested a back-office database application tailored to meet the needs of international nongovernmental organizations. Deployed the application and trained end users.

Analyzed, designed, developed and tested a subscription management database application for a charitable organization's regular publication.

April 1999–December 1999
Fellowship for African Relief
Khartoum, Sudan

PROGRAM DIRECTOR
Planned and executed humanitarian projects that targeted drought and war-affected people. Managed the daily operation of 2 nutrition clinics, 2 pit latrine construction workshops and an orphanage for abandoned newborns. Developed proposals for project funding and produced project reports for donors. Formulated administrative and field operations policies and procedures.

May 1994–March 1999
Company X (www.Company X.ca)
Mississauga, ON

PROJECT EXPERIENCE
Analyzed the effort to enhance a natural gas business transaction management system in response to a corporate merger, new industry standards and emerging technologies. Defined a project plan and budgetary cost estimate for development and deployment of the proposed system.

Analyzed, designed, coded, tested and deployed functional enhancements to a natural gas business transaction management system. These enhancements were a result of industry deregulation.

Designed, developed and deployed an OLAP application to forecast the availability of underground gas storage for a natural gas company using best-available actual and forecasted data.

September 1991–April 1994
Fellowship for African Relief
Khartoum, Sudan

DIRECTOR OF OPERATIONS
Planned and executed humanitarian projects that targeted drought-
and war-affected people. Managed the daily operation of 2 emergency
food distribution programs. Developed proposals for project funding
and produced project reports for donors. Formulated administrative
and field operations policies and procedures.

July 1986 – August 1991
Company X (www.Company X.ca)
Toronto, ON

Process engineering assignments including: plant engineering, process
modelling and development of plant operations simulation software for
the metals industry.

PROFESSIONAL AFFILIATIONS
Professional Engineers of Ontario
Project Management Institute

TECHNICAL SKILLS
Requirements analysis: QSS Doors
CASE tools: Oracle Designer
Relational database: Oracle RDBMS, Microsoft Access
Programming languages: SQL, PL/SQL
Development tools: SQL Navigator, NetTerm
Operating systems: IBM AIX, Windows
Project management: Microsoft Project
SDLC Methodologies: Rational Unified Process (RUP)

TRAINING
2004 Introduction to the Rational Unified Process
2003 Introduction to Six Sigma (Company X)
2003 Active Leadership Program (Company X)
2003 Negotiating Client Engagement (Company X)
2002 Oral Presentation Skills (Company X)
1999 Oracle8: New Features for Developers
1998 Web Developer Seminar
1998 Oracle Designer 2000 Workshop
1997 Oracle Financial Analyzer and Express OLAP Tools
1995 Oracle7 for Application Developers

1995 Tuning Oracle7 Server Applications
1995 Introduction to G2 Expert Systems

EDUCATION
1984–1986 M.A.Sc. in Chemical Engineering
University X (Windsor, ON) 1980–1984
B.A.Sc. in Chemical Engineering University X (Windsor, ON)

ENGINEERING RÉSUMÉ: AFTER

JUSTIN DALEY
321 Laurier Crescent, Toronto, ON K2P 3R5
(555) 555-8288 • jdaley@anyisp.com

SENIOR MANAGEMENT PROFESSIONAL
PROJECT MANAGEMENT / CONSULTING /
HUMANITARIAN PROJECTS

Dynamic manager with 20 years' experience co-ordinating successful programs in diverse and challenging environments worldwide. Proven track record combines expertise in process development, organizational leadership and project management with strong qualifications in systems development, written and oral communication, and problem-solving. Expert strategist, analyst, planner and project leader who has delivered concrete results in program deployment and implementation. Participative leadership style with well-developed skills in motivational team-building, quality performance and conflict management. Responds to challenges with confidence, determination and focus.

- Process and Procedure Development
- Report and Proposal Writing
- Project Management
- Tactical Planning
- Critical Problem-Solving and Analysis
- Leadership and Mentoring

- Client Relationship Management
- Product Development and Design
- Diplomacy and Cultural Sensitivity
- Communication and Presentations

Delivering Leadership Strategies, Boosting Productivity & Profitability

---

PROFESSIONAL EXPERIENCE:

COMPANY X—Mississauga, ON   **2000 to Present**
Project Systems Manager (February 2006 to Present)
Responsibilities include planning and co-ordinating tasks associated with IT infrastructure, engineering design tools and project management systems.
- Ensured success of capital project worth more than one billion dollars by managing team of specialists to establish and support technology required for execution of engineering, procurement and construction management activities.

Project Manager (May 2000 to Present)
Responsible for managing software application development and technology projects for internal and external clients.

- Solved technology and workload issues in newly-established Brazil office by managing resources on three continents to establish fully-functional project execution environment within 90 days.
- Succeeded in delivering state-of-the-art information system for client whose internal team's previous efforts had failed.
- Secured substantial new business for company by developing reputation for top-quality work delivered on time and within budget.

Program Manager—Program Management Office (November 2003 to October 2005)
Responsible for leading senior seven-member team in establishment of program management office to oversee information systems on major engineering, procurement and construction management projects.

- Raised quality of internal projects by using experience and training to establish standard project management practices based on quantifiable targets and quality reviews.
- Improved delivery of project execution systems on major capital projects with establishment of Project Systems Manager role.

Regional Director—North America (March 2002 to October 2005)
Responsibilities included development of business strategies, including co-ordination of resource utilization, defining and managing quality management system, and planning and participating in performance appraisals and career development process.

- Recognized for top management skills when chosen to lead Systems business unit and asked by company president to build relationship between Company X and Engineers Without Borders.
- Boosted morale and productivity by establishing appraisal/career development methodology recognized as best in organization.

INDEPENDENT CONSULTANT—Toronto, ON   **2000**
Project Consultant

- Fulfilled needs of international nongovernmental organizations with design, development and deployment of customized back-office database application and by training end users.
- Improved efficiency by analyzing, designing, developing and testing subscription management database application for charitable organization's regular publication.

FELLOWSHIP FOR AFRICAN RELIEF—Khartoum, Sudan　　1999
Program Director
Responsible for planning and executing humanitarian projects for drought-
and war-affected people, including operation of two nutrition clinics,
orphanage for abandoned newborns and pit latrine construction workshops.
- Cut resource requirements in half with design, development and
  implementation of database software application to manage
  human resources and finance functionality.
- Added value by including powerful reporting capability in design
  of above-mentioned database software application.
- Improved financial stability by developing proposals for project
  funding and producing project reports for donors.
- Ensured smooth operations by formulating administrative and
  field operations policies and procedures.

COMPANY X — Mississauga, ON　　　　　　　1994 to 1999
Software Specialist
Responsible for analyzing, designing, coding, testing and deploying
management systems and applications to assist various clients in
meeting industry challenges.
- Contributed to client success in face of corporate merger, new
  industry standards and emerging technologies by defining project
  plan and cost estimate for development and deployment of new
  transaction management system.
- Assisted client in adapting to industry deregulation by developing
  and deploying functional enhancements to a natural gas business
  transaction management system.
- Enhanced forecasting ability of client with design, development
  and deployment of OLAP application using best available actual
  and forecasted data to predict availability of underground gas
  storage.

FELLOWSHIP FOR AFRICAN RELIEF —
Khartoum, Sudan　　　　　　　　　　1991 to 1994
Director of Operations
Responsible for planning and executing humanitarian projects for
drought- and war-affected people including daily operation of two
emergency food distribution programs.

COMPANY X — Toronto, ON　　　　　　　　1986 to 1991
Process Engineer
Responsible for process engineering assignments including plant
engineering, process modelling and development of plant operations
simulation software for metals industry.

EDUCATION & TRAINING

M.A.Sc. (Chemical Engineering) — Windsor, ON	1986
B.A.Sc. (Chemical Engineering) — Windsor, ON	1984
Introduction to the Rational Unified Process, Toronto, ON	2004
Introduction to Six Sigma — Company X,Toronto, ON	2003
Active Leadership Program — Company X, Toronto, ON	2003
Negotiating Client Engagement — Company X, Toronto, ON	2003
Oral Presentation Skills — Company X, Toronto, ON	2002
Oracle8: New Features for Developers, Mississauga, ON	1999
Web Developer Seminar, Etobicoke, ON	1998
Oracle Designer 2000 Workshop, Vancouver, BC	1998
Oracle Financial Analyzer and Express OLAP Tools, Mississauga, ON	1997
Oracle7 for Application Developers, Mississauga, ON	1995
Tuning Oracle7 Server Applications, Mississauga, ON	1995
Introduction to G2 Expert Systems, Boston, MA	1995

AWARDS

Company X Award of Excellence — Company X, Mississauga, ON	2002

ASSOCIATIONS & AFFILIATIONS

Member: Professional Engineers of Ontario	1988 to Present
Member: Project Management Institute	2005 to Present
Chair: Board of Deacons, Church X, Toronto, ON	1998 to 1999

TECHNICAL SKILLS:

OS / Software: IBM AIX / Windows / Microsoft Office (Word, Excel, PowerPoint, Outlook)
Requirements Analysis: QSS Doors
CASE Tools: Oracle Designer
Relational Database: Oracle RDBMS / Microsoft Access
Programming Languages: SQL / PL/SQL
Development Tools: SQL Navigator / NetTerm
Project Management: Microsoft Project
SDLC Methodologies: Rational Unified Process (RUP)

Key Differences

- Professional experience was completely reformatted to make it flow better.
- A paragraph was added to list the key achievements, traits, skills and relevant experience to the position being applied for.
- Dates were added into the Associations and Affiliations section.
- Bullets were added to show the key skills that are relevant to the job and also based on experience in the past.
- The Training and Execution sections were reformatted to show dates at the right side, and the titles of the courses/training institutions were emphasized to make them stand out.

EXECUTIVE RÉSUMÉ: BEFORE

SUSAN SMITH
14 Robin Hood Drive, Toronto, ON M3P 1P5
(555) 555-5188 • ssmith@anyisp.com

Objective: To find work with a company, agency or association that appreciates my ability to Empower, Promote, Inspire and Communicate.

Education
1991   **College of Applied Arts and Technology**
Social Service Worker Diploma Program (S.S.W.)

Work Experience
2001–present   **C.E.O.**
The Chief Executive Officer is the senior staff person of the Amalgamated Appeal Organization and as such is responsible for the operational performance in the area. The primary functions of the position are achievement of implementing policies and avoiding non-compliance with the stated policies regarding unacceptable circumstances.

Responsibilities include:
Providing leadership in the development and achievement of the philosophy, mission and strategy and in the formulation of goals and objectives.
Providing communication with the membership at large to promote and inform the members about business issues.
Maintaining a public presence to raise the profile of the organization so that continuity exists from year to year.
Providing required monitoring reports on executive limitations.
Ensuring optimal communication between staff and the Board of Directors.
Developing agendas for meetings, as well as preparing the minutes of these meetings.
Ensuring that the Chair and Directors are kept fully informed of the condition of the organization and of all important factors influencing it.
Organizing and ensuring that the Committee structure of the organization functions effectively. Forming new committees where necessary and attending committee meetings.
Determining the strategic direction and annual business plans that result in the accomplishment of the Ends within the prescribed executive limitations.

Deciding the organizational structure and managing the staff, including recruitment, compensation and supervision.

Developing and instituting processess and procedures to manage all aspects of the business.

Acting as the representative of the organization to the public and media.

Continually developing skills to lead and direct the organization.

Providing direction for the membership sales team and monitoring membership development.

Following committee progress and ensuring that regular reports are on permanent record.

Arranging for representation in the community where necessary.

Ensuring high visibility of the organization within the business community, articles to the local media, etc.

Maintaining liaison with other members and business organizations.

Researching information on the business community as requested.

Having full understanding of the financial management of the organization, making recommendations as requested.

Overseeing the maintenance of the accounting system, database and files.

Taking responsibility for the planning, implementation and administration of programs and membership services, together with committee chairpersons.

Overseeking and planning content of the newsletter and the Membership Directory.

Attending CEO/Manager training annually.

1997–2001   **Executive Director**
Responsible for interviewing, hiring, supervising, scheduling and training of 4 receptionists who staff switchboard after hours and weekends; 30 volunteers to staff Community Information Centre Phones payroll; accounts payable, marketing, database development/management; liaison with Staff; community liaison; scheduling, organizing/attending Board Meetings, Volunteer Meetings and Special Events.

Facts of Interest:
1996–1999   Business Owner, Facilitator, True Colors™ Level 1 Trainer, facilitation of 6-week course/evening seminars/seasonal retreats for women wanting to make changes in their lives. Topics included Goal Setting, Attitude, Self-Awareness, Networking, Visualization & Affirmations.

1982–1995   Owner and Operator, Daycare for children, 6 months to 12 years of age.

1995–present   Founding and current member of Targets, a women's networking and support group.

EXECUTIVE RÉSUMÉ: AFTER

SUSAN SMITH
14 Robin Hood Drive, Toronto, O'
(555) 555-5188 • ssmith@anyisp.

MANAGEMENT PROFESSIONAL
LEADERSHIP / PROJECT MANAGEMENT / MARKETING
Governments, Community Agencies & Not-For-Profit Organizations

Dynamic, senior business leader with strong experience spearheading successful ventures and implementing business innovations. Expert strategist, analyst, planner, team leader and negotiator who has delivered dramatic gains in revenues, profits and organizational profile. Extensive network of connections within social service and nonprofit agencies, corporate community and governments at municipal and regional levels. Participative leadership style with excellent skills in cross-functional team building, quality performance and productivity improvement. Responds to business challenges with confidence, determination and focus.

- Community Work & Organization
- Information & Research
- Recruitment & Advocacy
- Resource Allocation
- Teamwork & Interaction

- Volunteer Management
- Critical Analysis & Problem-Solving
- Marketing & Event Planning
- Written & Oral Communications
- Facilitation & Motivation

Delivering Leadership Strategies Driving Productivity & Performance

---

PROFESSIONAL EXPERIENCE:
AMALGAMATED APPEAL   **2001 to Present**
Chief Executive Officer
Responsible for operational performance by running programs, formulating goals and objectives and providing leadership in development and achievement of philosophy mission and strategy.

- Raised organizational profile by meeting regularly with local and regional officials as well as attending conferences with local officials.
- Widened exposure of organization through initiatives as well as creating business card, flyer and member product showcase areas from underutilized office space.
- Boosted communication abilities with minimal cost by researching and upgrading copier system, allowing in-house printing of monthly newsletter.

- Increased productivity and performance with implementation of new Internet-based database and calendar and establishment of Office Procedure Manual, ensuring awareness of best practices used elsewhere.

INFORMATION TORONTO, Toronto, ON   **1997 to 2001**
Executive Director
Responsible for interviewing, hiring, supervising, scheduling and training four staff receptionists and 10 telephone volunteers.
- Raised organizational profile through liaison with community at large and staff.
- Strengthened role of volunteers by developing a Community Information and Volunteer Centre, using experience and contacts gained through membership in Volunteer Canada.
- Developed and implemented, as a key team member, a large event to celebrate International Year of the Volunteer.
- Contributed to organizational success by organizing and participating in volunteer meetings and special events.
- Ensured smooth day-to-day operations by performing payroll, accounts payable, marketing and database development duties.

INDEPENDENT CONTRACTOR, Toronto, ON   **1982 to 1999**
Business Owner / Facilitator (1996 to 1999)
Responsible for training and facilitating courses, seminars and retreats for women wanting to make life changes on topics including Goal Setting, Attitude, Self-Awareness, Networking, Visualization and Affirmations.

Owner / Operator (1982 to 1995)
Responsible for all aspects of running business and caring for children aged six months to twelve years.

EDUCATION & TRAINING

Coursework, Social Service Worker Program	**1991**
Certified Sales Professional Professional Sales Association, Toronto, ON	**2003**
Certified Information and Referral Specialist	**2000**
Fundamentals in Management of Volunteers	**2000**
Emergency Measures of Ontario Certificate of Achievement	**1999**
Level 1 True Colors Trainer	**1999**
Citizens Awareness Program Certificate — X Regional Police, ON	**1999**
The G.O.S.T. Planning Process	**1997**
Coaching Skills for Managers	**1997**
Mediating Interpersonal Conflict	**1997**

AWARDS
Business Achievement Award

SOFTWARE:
MS Office (Word, Excel, PowerPoint, Access, Outlook)

Key Differences

- A paragraph was added to list key achievements, traits, skills and experience relevant to the position being applied for.
- The Facts of Interest section was incorporated into the Education and Training section.
- The Education section was moved from the top of the résumé to the bottom and reformatted.
- The company name and role for each past job were emphasized to make them easier to read.
- The Professional Experience section was reformatted and is much clearer and easier to read.

BEYOND WORKOPOLIS.COM, WORKING.COM AND MONSTER.CA:
OTHER JOB WEBSITES TO VISIT

GENERAL

Acti Job
www.actijob.nicejob.ca

All Canadian Jobs
www.allcanadianjobs.com

All Star Jobs
www.allstarjobs.ca

Canada Jobs
www.canadajobs.com

Can Jobs
www.canjobs.com

Canadian Job Bank
jb-ge.hrdc-drhc.gc.ca

Canuck Careers
www.canuckcareers.com

Career Beacon
www.careerbeacon.com

Career Builder
www.headhunter.net

EmployCanada
www.employcanada.com

EmployXpress
www.exployxpress.com

Yahoo Hot Jobs Canada
www.hotjobs.ca

Job Island
www.ca.jobisland.com

Job Shark
www.jobshark.com

Job Boom
www.jobboom.com

Monster.ca (Canada)
www.monster.ca

PlusJobs Canada
www.canada.plusjobs.com/fronteng.shtml

The Work Place—Canadian Government Resources
www.theworkplace.ca

Workopolis
www.workopolis.com

Work Destinations — Canadian Relocation and Regulated Jobs
www.workdestinations.org

Employment News
www.employmentnews.com

Working Canada
www.working.canada.com

ACADEMIC/EDUCATION

Apply To Teach Network
www.attn.org

Education Canada Network
www.educationcanada.com

Career.edu
www.career.edu

AGRICULTURE

Agricultural Institute of Canada
www.aic.ca/careers.cfm

AG Careers
www.agcareers.com

ARTS, CULTURE & NEW MEDIA

BackstageJobs.com
www.backstagejobs.com/jobs.htm

Culture Works
www.cultureworks.ca/jobs/index.asp

Work in Culture
www.workinculture.on.ca

AVIATION/AEROSPACE

AVCanada
www.avcanada.ca

AVIANation—Aviation Jobs Worldwide
www.avianation.com

Space Careers
www.space-careers.com/jobsearch.html

BUSINESS MANAGEMENT/EXECUTIVE

Canadian Association of Supply Chain and Logistics
Management
www.infochain.org/jobs/jobops.html

Canadian Payroll Association: Job Connect
www.payroll.ca/English/JobConnect/jce.htm

Executive Listings
www.exec-appointments.com

Job Wings — Finance, Accounting, Management
www.jobwings.com

Purchasing Management Association of Canada — Employment
Referral Service
www.pmac.ca/ERS.htm

CHARITABLE/NON-PROFIT SECTOR

Action Without Borders
www.idealist.org/career

Charity Village
www.charityvillage.com

Human Rights Job Board
www.hri.ca/jobboard

Charity Job Search
www.charityjobsearch.com

ENVIRONMENT/GEOLOGICAL

Canadian Enviro Jobs
www.canadianenvironmental.com/envirojobs

CCHREI Job Board
www.cchrei.ca

Environmental Jobs and Careers
www.ecoemploy.com/noindex/bypmap.html

Forestry Employment Bulletin Board
www.canadian-forests.com/job.html

Geological Association of Canada — Geosciences
www.gac.ca/GAC/jobs.htm

Geomatics Canada
www.geomaticscanada.com/jobs.cfm

FINANCE

Accounting
www.accountingjobs.ca
Certified General Accountants
www.cgajobs.org

Certified Management Accountants
www.cma-canada.org

Finance
www.financejobs.ca

Investment
www.moneyjobs.ca

Job Wings — Finance, Accounting, Management
www.jobwings.com

GOVERNMENT

Canadian Municipalities
www.theworkplace.ca

Federal Public Service Commission of Canada
www.jobs-emplois.gc.ca/jobs/index_all_e.htm

Government of Alberta
www.pao.gov.ab.ca/jobs

Government of British Columbia
www.employment.gov.bc.ca

Government of Manitoba
www.gov.mb.ca/csc/employment/jobs.html

Government of New Brunswick
www.ere.gnb.ca/competition.aspx

Government of Newfoundland and Labrador
www.psc.gov.nl.ca/psc/jobs/entry.htm

Government of Northwest Territories
www.hr.gov.nt.ca/employment

Government of Nova Scotia
www.gov.ns.ca/careers

Government of Nunavut
www.gov.nu.ca/Nunavut

Government of Ontario
www.gojobs.gov.on.ca

Government of Prince Edward Island
www.gov.pe.ca/jobs

Government of Quebec
www.tresor.gouv.qc.ca/fr/ress_humaine/emplois/liste_emplois/
liste.asp

Government of Saskatchewan
www.gov.sk.ca/psc

Government of Yukon
www.employment.gov.yk.ca

HEALTH CARE/MEDICAL/PARA-MEDICAL

Canadian Association of Speech-Language Pathologists and
Audiologists
www.caslpa.ca/english/careers/ads.asp

Canadian Medical Placement Service
www.cmps.ca

Canadian Society for Epidemiology and Biostatistics
www.cseb.ca/en/employment.htm

Canadian Society for International Health Job Opportunities
www.csih.org/en/opportunities/jobopps.asp

MedHunters
www.medhunters.com

Medical Job Search
www.medicaljobsearch.ca/search.php

Nursing Employment Directory
www.canadianrn.com/jobmart/newjobs.htm

Ontario Physician Job Registry
www.pairoregistry.com

Opticians Association of Canada
www.opticians.ca/professionals/classifieds.asp

Pharmahorizons
www.pharmahorizons.com

Physical Therapy Jobs
www.ptjobs.com

HOSPITALITY/FOOD SERVICES

Canadian Institute of Travel Counsellors
www.citc.ca/content/en/about-employment-e.asp

Cool Jobs Canada
www.cooljobscanada.com

Hospitality Careers.ca
www.hcareers.ca

Tourism Work Web
www.tourismworkweb.com

JOURNALISM/MEDIA/PUBLIC RELATIONS

Canadian Newspaper Association
www.cna-acj.ca/careers
Canadian Public Relations Society
www.pub-rels.com

Graphic Designers of Canada
www.gdc.net/community/job_board.php

Jeff Gaulin's Journalism Job Board
www.jeffgaulin.com

Masthead — Magazine Industry
www.mastheadonline.com/job.htm

Media Job Search Canada
www.mediajobsearchcanada.ca

MilkMan Unlimited (radio)
www.milkmanunlimited.ca

Playback Magazine
www.playbackmag.com

Canadian Magazine Publishers Association — Career Centre
www.cmpa.ca/jobs/jobshead.html

LAW ENFORCEMENT/MILITARY/PEACEKEEPING

Canadian Border Services Agency
www.cbsa-asfc.gc.ca/careers

Canadian Forces Recruiting
www.recruiting.forces.gc.ca

RCMP Recruiting
www.rcmp-grc.gc.ca

United Nations Jobs Site
www.jobs.un.org/Galaxy/Release3/vacancy/vacancy.aspx

LEGAL

Canadian Corps of Commissionaires
www.commissionaires.ca

Legal Job Board
www.legaljobboard.ca

MARKETING/COMMUNICATIONS

Advertising Age
www.adage.com

CPRS Career File
www.pub-rels.com

Marketing Magazine
www.marketingmag.ca

Strategy Magazine
www.strategymag.com

RETAIL

CanadianRetail.com
www.canadianretail.com

Cool Jobs Canada
www.cooljobscanada.com

Grocery Industry Job Board
www.cfig.ca/jobboard/jobboard.asp

SOCIOLOGY/SOCIAL WORK

Canadian Sociology and Anthropology Association
www.artsci-ccwin.concordia.ca/socanth/CSAA/jobs.htm

Social Worker Action Team
www.swatjobs.com

SPORTS/LEISURE

Canadian Sport
www.canadiansport.com/jobs

Leisure Information Network
www.lin.ca

TECHNOLOGY/ENGINEERING

BC Technology
www.bctechnology.com/frameset_emp.html

Canada ComputerWork
www.canada.computerwork.com

Canada IT
www.canadait.com

Canadian Technical Employment Network
www.cten.ca

Engineering Central
www.engcen.com/JobSearch.asp

IT Harvest
www.itharvest.com/job.cfm?task=search

IT Job Universe
www.itjobuniverse.ca

NetJobs
www.netjobs.com

PositionWatch
www.positionwatch.com

INTERNATIONAL

International Jobs & Relocation
www.escapeartist.com

Riley Guide — International Employment
www.rileyguide.com/internat.html

ACKNOWLEDGEMENTS

T he concept for this book originated eight years ago, at a breakfast meeting with an individual who is now a good friend —
Robert Ferguson, founder of The Knowledge Marketing Group. He
planted the seed and kept pouring water and sunshine on these ideas.
Thanks, Robert, for your persistence!

They say it takes a village to raise a child; I believe the same can be
said for a book. I wish to thank the following people: Kim Peters,
Debbie Trenholm, Joanna Track, Jen Riley, Andrew Stewart, Sean
Pronger, Eric Morse, John Stanton, Leonard Lee, Diane Francis,
Sebastian Managò, Catherine Hajanal, William Jans, Peter Jensen,
Paul Henderson and Zacary Houle. Your insights and suggestions
were invaluable.

Special thanks go to Michael Garner, who collaborated with me on
The Canadian Job Search Kit. Many of the principles and words in
this book first came to life on that project. *Get the Right Job, Right
Now!* could not have been written without his original input.

This book is based in large part on lessons I have learned from a
number of people that I have been fortunate to work with. These
are the people who have mentored me in my career and who have
helped shape my thinking about work: Perry Stiegner, Frank Sims,
Steve Cook, Peter Ward, Patrick Galpin, Frank Vrabel and Mike
Marsden. Special thanks to Craig Bisset, who saw my potential, supported me and believed in me. When Craig opened the door at Ward
Associates, he not only provided me with a job in the amazing world

of career management; he also put me on the path that led me to my life's purpose. I am eternally grateful.

Thanks to my team, who assisted with the editing and research to help create this book: Cheryl Bonhomme, Debora Dekok, Tudor Robins, Anna Pasquale, Tracey Coveart, Monique Lugli, Lisa Rogers, Kim Bernier, Lynn Shortt, Cameron Whalen and Eunice Moyer. Special thanks to Carol Gregson and Kevin Schafer, who provided support when I really needed it.

To the hundreds of clients who have given me and my team the privilege of being involved in one of the most important parts of their lives, I thank you. We are continually inspired by your courage to renounce the status quo and to get the most out of your careers and your lives.

I want to thank my dear friends Dean Jackson, James and Julie Dietrich, and Al and Sheri Doseger for their lifelong friendship. I also want to extend my gratitude to Walter and Charlotte Leopkey for their warm hospitality, the prairie air, the porch and the wide-open view — a great place to think and write!

The team at HarperCollins has been a pleasure to work with, from the editors to the designers and the sales team. Special thanks go to Noelle Zitzer, and particularly to Senior Editor Brad Wilson, who originally approached me to do the book. (When it is your first book, you have no clue how to start!) Brad saw the potential and had a very clear vision of what this book could become; he was the key person who brought all of the pieces together. Brad, your leadership is a true example of what a professional can do for a project like this one.

Thanks to my family — to my parents for having the courage not to settle, the strength to leave the comfort of what you knew to pursue your dreams in Canada. Your commitment to doing your best, no matter what the task, is a true inspiration. I'm grateful to you for showing me that work can be meaningful and full of joy.

Thanks to my children, Aine and Aidan, for being so patient over those weekends and nights as I worked on completing this project. You two amaze me with your talent, creativity and passion — what more could a dad ask for?

To Yvonne, you are the most all-around talented person that I know. You continually inspire me in so many ways — with your loyalty, your passion for excellence and your independent spirit. You carried an extra load at home while I finished this book, and I thank you with my whole heart.

And finally, to God be the glory.

INDEX

NOTES